T0149751

THE
MODERN-DAY
CYRUS

Rev. Robert Antwi

authorHOUSE®

AuthorHouse™
1663 Liberty Drive
Bloomington, IN 47403
www.authorhouse.com
Phone: 1 (800) 839-8640

Published by AuthorHouse 06/14/2018

ISBN: 978-1-5462-4715-9 (sc)
ISBN: 978-1-5462-4714-2 (e)

Library of Congress Control Number: 2018907029

Print information available on the last page.

Scripture taken from The Holy Bible, King James Version. Public Domain

CONTENTS

Acknowledgments

I give glory and honor to God for the strength and wisdom given to me to accomplish this task. I am very grateful for getting this book published. I thank my coworkers at 8401 Rising Sun, Philadelphia, for the encouragement and the support they gave me.

Thank you to Miss Anissa Bane, the CTM, Sharkerah Wallace, Tyreek Reaves, Washington Kimber, Benjamin Makor, Damien Mosley, Brandon Miles, Nyjah Lindsey, Reginald Payne, and all the replacement staff members who come to 8401 to give a helping hand. I could not have completed this project without your support.

I would like also to thank my kids, especially Jedidah Owusu Asimeng Antwi who has been praying with me and following me to Mama Rosemond's Harvest Fellowship International, my spiritual mother. I will like to give a big thank you to my spiritual mother, Mama Rosemond. She has been praying for me, and I love the ministry that God has called her into. Mama Ivy and Samuel Asamoah, may the Lord Jesus grant you your heart's desire for your kindness toward me. Finally, may the Lord bless you all and my faithful family in Yeadon, Pennsylvania.

INTRODUCTION

The Almighty God uses the things that are despised by man to do magnificent things so that all glory will go to the Father and Creator of heaven and earth. How could Donald Trump beat an seasoned politician and former secretary of state, Hillary Clinton to become the forty-fifth President of the United States of America?

Since the US elections in 2016, I have been wondering how it happened. I bought into the idea of the Russian collusion, but I believed otherwise. I could see Donald Trump tackling issues that no man dared to even talk about. Some of the bold initiatives taken by Donald Trump were overhauling the US tax system, declaring Jerusalem the capital of Israel on December 6, 2017, and intending to move the US embassy from Tel Aviv to Jerusalem. To me, this is a remarkable achievement. I believe this is the reason why God brought Donald Trump to power.

I do not agree with all the policies of Donald Trump, but for this one, he got it right. I am an immigrant from Ghana, and I have been in the United States for twenty years without a green card. I have a master's in business administration with a concentration in finance from Haub School of Business at Saint Joseph University in Philadelphia and a master's in divinity from Palmer Theological Seminary from Eastern University Saint Davids Pennsylvania.

I work with Merakey (NHS) and minister at Harvest

Fellowship International in New Jersey. I do not like Donald Trump's policy on immigration, but this will not let me attest to the fact that Donald Trump was elected president by the acts of God.

When I was young, I did not know anything about Tel Aviv. I thought Israel's capital was Jerusalem until I got to high School. Prempeh College is an Ivy League school in Kumasi, Ghana. I studied geography and got to know that Tel Aviv was the capital of Israel. I began wondering why the leaders of this great nation, Israel, had not changed the capital from Tel Aviv to Jerusalem. If Nigeria could change its capital from Lagos to Abuja, why couldn't Israel?

As I grew up, I got to know about the tension in the Middle East and how Jerusalem had been the center of contention between the Jews and the Arabs. I prayed for the day Jerusalem would be declared the capital of Israel. I thank God for being alive to see this day.

Whether you like it or not, the Jewish people are election of God. If you touch them, you touch the apple of God's eyes. Look at history. Many nations oppressed Israel, slaughtering God's people—but they would come out stronger and more refined.

I will use the Word of God to show how Donald Trump is a modern-day Cyrus.

1

WHO IS KING CYRUS?

King Cyrus was born in Anshan, Iran, in 600 BC, and he died in 530 BC. He lived for seventy years and was one of the most powerful and greatest kings of all time. He was known as Cyrus II of Persia, or Cyrus the Great, but the Greeks called him Cyrus the Elder. He was affectionately called the Father in the Persian Empire, for he was kind and treated everyone with respect. He was a good ruler who was loved by his people. He was the founder of the Achaemenid Empire, which was the first Persian Empire.

The book of Isaiah, written around 800 BC, gave a prophecy about this great king. Bible scholars had divided Isaiah into three parts. It is believed that the first part was written by Isaiah, but the second and third parts were likely written by different authors. No matter how you may think about it, I believe the book of Isaiah was written by Isaiah Ben Amoz of Jerusalem, the son of Amoz. Isaiah was written around 800 BC, and Cyrus the Great was born around 600 BC.

It took almost two hundred years for the prophecy of Isaiah to be fulfilled. It is said that the mother of Cyrus, Mandane of Medea, died after Cyrus was born, and Cyrus's father, Cambyses Kanbujiya, was a small king of the Persians. Cyrus was trained to be a shepherd.

He grew up among highlanders who believed themselves superior to the inhabitants of the Plain beneath them. That was not the actual truth, but all mountain people shared the belief. Then too, he became accustomed to horseback at the age of five or six, when lowland boys still made toys of clay, dried by the canal banks. With his cousins, both boys and girls, he climbed to the bare back of a horse, the children holding on by the mane or gripping each other. They saw at once that only captives or Old People walked afoot.[1]

He rode his horse like a king, and he thought of himself as a son of a great king. He studied at the king's gate. The students knew nothing about written words, so they relied on the spoken words from their teachers. At a young age, Cyrus thought that he was Aryan, a horse rider, and a conqueror.

> The prophet Isaiah prophesied about Cyrus two hundred years before he was born says, "That saith of Cyrus, He is my shepherd, and shall perform all my pleasure: even saying to Jerusalem, Thou shalt be built: and to the temple, Thy foundation shall be laid." (Isaiah 44:28)

This was a prophecy of precision since Cyrus was trained to be a shepherd. This prophecy called Cyrus "my shepherd" and gave the precise mission of what Cyrus was going to do: he was to build Jerusalem, which would be destroyed by Nebuchadnezzar, and he was to lay the foundation of

---

[1] Harold Lamb, *Cyrus the Great* (Garden City, NY: Doubleday and Company), 14.

the temple, which was laid when Cyrus was the king (but it had to be finished during the reign of Darius). Cyrus died after the foundation of the temple was laid. Cyrus would also do what pleases God by setting God's people free from captivity.

God spoke to the Israelites during the exodus from Egypt to the Promised Land. He told them that the city in which He would place His name should be their center of worship or the capital.

> But unto the place which the Lord your God shall choose out of all your tribes to put his name there, even unto his habitation shall ye seek, and thither thou shall come. (Deuteronomy 12:5)

The place where the Lord God would put his name is repeated several times in Deuteronomy. God placed His name on Jerusalem during the reign of King David.

> God says, "But I have chosen Jerusalem that my name might be there; and have chosen David to be over my people Israel." (2 Chronicles 6:6)

Two hundred years later, around 1000 BC—and before Isaiah came into the picture—Jerusalem became the capital of Israel. The election of the Hebrews, the Jewish people, was providential since people had no time for God their Creator. Instead they were living their own lives as it pleased them.

Life in the ancient days was similar to today. Many people have no time for God, but they have time for the almighty dollar. If you have no time for God, then God will also have no time for you. God did not create us like robots. He gave us free will. God expects us to surrender our will to Him, serve Him, and glorify Him. God will protect us from all spiritual forces that rise against us. God will fight our battles for us, provide for our needs, and honor us with long life, well-being, and prosperity.

> Praise ye the Lord, Blessed is the man that feareth the Lord, that delighteth greatly in his commandments. His seed shall be mighty upon the earth: the generation of the upright shall be blessed. Wealth and riches shall be in his house: and his righteousness endureth for ever. Unto the upright there ariseth light in the darkness: he is gracious, and full of compassion, and righteous. (Psalm 112:1–3)

If you trust in the Lord and abide by the Word of God, then your children are going to be great in this world. Your generation will be blessed. You will not see your children in police cells or in prisons. Your children will never do anything that is against the laws of the land where they live. Your children are going to be prosperous and live healthy lives.

Your children will grow to know the Lord and live their lives according to the Word of God. Also, wealth and riches will be in your house. This means one can be rich and not wealthy, while another person can be wealthy and not rich. To be rich means you have money, funds, cash, assets, capital resources, or reserves. When one is wealthy, then the person has an abundance of valuable possessions, affluence, prosperity, riches, means, substance, and fortune. It is the state of being rich—material prosperity. Therefore, the wealthy person has lands, factories, companies, cars, boats, jet planes, equipment, and much more. It is the desire of God to make you rich so that you can help in building the kingdom of God. God will direct you to a path of wealth and riches.

> Thus saith the Lord, thy Redeemer, the Holy One of Israel; I am the Lord thy God which teacheth thee to profit, which leadeth thee by the way that thou shouldest go. (Isaiah 48:17)

God will teach you to profit, which means God will show you the things that you should do to get rich.

God is going to lead you to the way you should go. Many Christians are poor because they do not seek direction in life from God. A Christian may study very hard to be a medical doctor, but that may not be where God wants the person to be. I did not know Jesus Christ as my Savior and Lord, so I studied to be a mining engineer. My intention was to steal gold and diamonds and enrich myself overnight, but that was not the will of God for me. I could not secure a job in the mines after graduation.

As I was sleeping one night, I heard a sermon about Jesus Christ. The preacher in my little village, Asokore, invited anyone to come to church to meet Jesus. I was going through hard times, and I decided to go to the church to give Jesus a try.

I went to the church and was converted on August 12, 1984. I've never regretted my decision. The door opened for me to secure a job as a mining supervisor with Ghana

5

Consolidated Diamonds, and I worked there for three years without stealing a speck of a diamond.

I prayed, and God told me that He wanted me to be a "miner of men" in the same way Jesus said to the fishermen that they would be fishers of men. Peter and Andrew knew what it meant to be fishers. I knew what it meant to be a miner.

I left the mines to study at the Apostolic Bible College in Kolding, Demark, for a year, and I then entered into ministry. If you trust in God and abide by the Word of God, there will be light arising when you are in the dark. That means God will see you through this dark world and be there for you in your dark days or horrible days. God is prepared to see us through the horrible days; God will never leave us or forsake us. He will also protect us from any harm.

> But now thus saith the Lord, that created thee, O Jacob, and he that form thee, O Israel, Fear not: for I have redeemed thee, I have called thee by thy name; thou art mine. When thou passest through the waters, I will be with thee; and through the rivers, they shall not overflow thee; when thou walkest through the fire thou shalt not be burned; neither shalt the flame kindle upon thee. For I am the Lord thy God, the Holy One of Israel, thy Saviour: I gave Egypt for thy ransom, Ethiopia and Seba for thee. Since thou was precious in my sight, thou has been honourable, and I have love thee: therefore will I give men for thee, and people for thy life. (Isaiah 43:1–4)

God is telling you not to be afraid. This way, you will be free from depression, confusion, and anxiety. Why? Because you belong to God. When you pass through the waters, God is going to be with you. There are innumerable problems in this world, and you will face numerous problems. You will never commit suicide because God will be with you through every day of your life. You will walk through the fire, but the fire will not burn you.

In a very difficult situation, you will be able to stand and get through it because God is watching over His Word to perform it. When the enemy attacks you, he will not succeed because God will fight the battle for you.

> So shall they fear name of the Lord from the west, and his glory from the rising of the sun. When the enemy shall come in like a flood, the Spirit of the Lord shall lift up a standard against him. (Isaiah 59:19)

The Bible does not promise a worry-free life. The Bible says the enemy will come in like a flood, which means Satan will come against you with destructive force. The Holy Spirit will lift a standard against the enemy. The difference between a Christian and an unbeliever is that the Christian has the Holy Spirit to fight life battles for him or her, and the unbeliever has no one to fight his or her battles.

Many people commit suicide because they can't stand the enemy. The enemy might talk to them—or they hear voices. They might get to the point where they are doing the bidding of the devil. The devil will tell them not to forgive their mothers or fathers for what they have done. They are not prepared to forgive.

The enemy may tell you to shoot someone—and you

7

will do the bidding of the devil. If you are a Christian who is hearing voices, be careful and look for a mighty woman or man of God to deliver you from the torment of the devil. Otherwise, you will do the bidding of the devil. The devil will tell you to commit suicide, and you will do it. It is better to be a Christian than an unbeliever.

During the time of Abraham, many people did not want anything to do with God. Abraham had favor with God. He found favor in the eyes of God, and God decided to bless him.

> Now the Lord has said unto Abram, get thee out of thy country, and from thy kindred, and from thy father's house, unto the land that I will shew thee: And I will make of thee a great nation, and I will bless thee, and make thy name great; and thou shalt be a blessing: And I will bless them that bless thee, and curse him that curseth thee: and in thee shall all families of the earth be blessed. (Genesis 12:1–3)

Abram was seventy-five years old when God spoke to him. Abram left Haran, the city of his father, Terah. God changed Abram's name to Abraham, which means "father of many nations." The descendants of Abraham are the present-day Israelites. God is the creator of heaven and earth, and He is not a man to go against His Word. God is faithful and has the power to perform all that he has spoken. He blessed Abraham and his descendants. Whether we like it or not, Israel is blessed. God said to the Israelites, "If you disobey me, you will go into captivity."

They disobeyed God several times and went into

captivity. During the Babylonian captivity, Isaiah gave a prophecy that Cyrus was going to be king. God would use Cyrus to bring the Israelites back to rebuild Jerusalem, the temple, and the nation. Although Cyrus did not know God—he was a heathen king—God used him to fulfill God's purpose. Isaiah said that Cyrus would get to know God through the mission assigned to him. The world would know that God could use anyone to do God's pleasure.

How and why did the Israelites go into the Babylonian captivity? Due to disobedience to God, Isaiah and Jeremiah both prophesied that the king of Babylon would take the Jews into captivity.

> Then said Isaiah to Hezekiah, Hear the word of the Lord of hosts: behold, the days come, that all that is in thine house, and that which thy fathers have laid up in store until this day, shall be carried to Babylon: nothing shall be left, saith the Lord. And of thy sons that shall issue from thee, which thou shall begat, shall they take away; they shall be eunuchs in the palace of the king of Babylon. (Isaiah 39:5–7)

To fulfill the prophecy, the Israelites were carried away into Babylonian captivity. This account can be found in Jeremiah 38 and 39. The Israelites disobeyed God, especially the last king of Judah. King Zedekiah believed the false prophets were pronouncing peace on Jerusalem in spite of the sins and atrocities that were going on in Judah. Jeremiah, the young prophet, was persecuted and nearly killed before God delivered him.

Pushur was the chief governor in the house of God. He

beat the prophet Jeremiah and put Jeremiah in the stocks that were in the high gate near the house of the Lord.

The next day, Jeremiah prophesied against Pushur and all his friends. He said King Nebuchadnezzar would take them into captivity because their unholy attitude toward God.

Jeremiah accused Pushur of being a false prophet.

King Zedekiah knew Jeremiah was a good prophet and secretly called Jeremiah to hear the Word of God.

Jeremiah told the king that God had delivered Judah into the hands of King Nebuchadnezzar. Jeremiah told Zedekiah to surrender to Nebuchadnezzar so that Jerusalem would not be burned. Zedekiah would eat at the table of Nebuchadnezzar until his death. King Zedekiah said the people would mock him, and he did not surrender.

It is sad that so many Christians are living to please people and not to please God or abiding by the Word of God. It is so pathetic. If you do not live your life according to the Word of God, you will not see God in the final days.

> Then Zedekiah the king sent, and took Jeremiah the prophet unto him into the third entry that is in the house of the Lord; and the king said unto Jeremiah, I will ask thee a thing; hide nothing from me. Then Jeremiah said unto Zedekiah, if I declare it unto thee, wilt thou not surely put me to death? And If I give thee counsel, wilt thou not hearken unto me? So Zedekiah the king sware secretly unto Jeremiah, saying, As the Lord liveth, that made us this soul, I will not put thee to death, neither will I give thee into the hands of these men that seek thy life. Then said

Jeremiah unto Zedekiah, Thus saith the Lord, the God of hosts, the God of Israel; If thou wilt assuredly go forth unto the king of Babylon's princes, then thou soul shall live, and this city shall not be burned with fire; and thou shalt live, and thine house; But if thou wilt not go forth to the king of Babylon' princes, then shall this city be given into the hand of the Chaldeans, and they shall burn it with fire, and thou shalt not escape out of their hand. And Zedekiah the king said unto Jeremiah, I am afraid of the Jews that are fallen to the Chaldeans, lest they deliver me into their hand, and they mock me. But Jeremiah said, They shall not deliver thee. Obey, I beseech thee, the voice of the Lord, which I speak unto thee: so it shall be well unto thee, and thy soul shall live. But if thou refuse to go forth, this is the word that the Lord hath shewed me: And, behold, all the women that are left in the king of Judah's house shall be brought forth to the king of Babylon's princes, and those women shall say, Thy friends have set thee on, and have prevailed against thee: thy feet are sunk in the mire, and they are turned away back. So they shall bring out all thy wives and thy children to the Chaldeans: and thou shalt not escape out of their hand, but shalt be taken by the hand of the king of Babylon: and thou shalt cause this city to be burned with fire. (Jeremiah 38:14–23)

I pray that I will not be afraid of what people are going to do or say about me and that I will be able to do the will of God without any intimidation. Zedekiah did not obey the Word of the Lord because he was afraid of people. The king's foolishness caused Jerusalem to be burned. It is arrogant and stupid to go against the Word of God. God, help me obey your Word. Whenever I fall short, strengthen me so that I will be able to do your will.

The fear of people is a trap for anyone who will give in. Stand firm for the Lord. Zedekiah refused the Word of God—and look what happened to him and the whole of Judah. In the ninth year of Zedekiah, the Babylonians came and encamped against the city of Jerusalem. In the eleventh year of King Zedekiah, the Babylonians broke the walls and marched into Jerusalem. Zedekiah had two years to repent and surrender to Nebuchadnezzar, but he did not.

When the princess broke the wall, Zedekiah tried to escape. He was caught. His wives were taken away from him, his children were slain before his very eyes, and the nobles of Judah were slain. The eyes of Zedekiah were taken out, his hands were put in handcuffs, and he was put in prison till he died.

> In the ninth year of Zedekiah king of Judah, in the tenth month, came Nebuchadnezzar king of Babylon and all his army against Jerusalem, and besieged it. And in the eleventh year of Zedekiah, in the fourth month, the city was broken up. And all the princes of the king of Babylon came in, and sat in the middle gate, even Nergalsharezer, Samgarnebo, Sarsechim, Rabsaris, Nergalsharezer, Rabmag, with

all the residue of the princes of the king of Babylon. And it came to pass, that when Zedekiah the king of Judah saw them, and all the men of war, then they fled, and went out of the city by night, by the way of the king's garden, by the gate betwixt the two walls, and he went out the way of the plain. But the Chaldeans' army pursued after them, and overtook Zedekiah in the plains of Jericho: and when they had taken him, they brought him up to Nebuchadnezzar king of Babylon to Riblah in the land of Hamath, where he gave judgment upon him. Then the king of Babylon slew the sons of Zedekiah in Riblah before his eyes: also the king of Babylon slew all the nobles of Judah. Moreover he put out Zedekiah's eyes, and bound him with chains, to carry him to Babylon. And the Chaldeans burned the king's house, and the houses of the people, with fire, and brake down the walls of Jerusalem. (Jeremiah 39:1–8)

We cannot trust in God and live any kind of life we want. We have to live by the Word of God. Zedekiah lost his wives, sons, nobles of Judah, and the throne. Jerusalem was burned because Zedekiah did not obey the Word of God. His eyes were taken out and bound in chains.

Many Christians' spiritual eyes are taken out, and they are bound in chains because of sin. We need to obey the Word of God to see with our spiritual eyes and know what God wants us to do. Many pastors amass wealth and live in million-dollar mansions and ride in flamboyant cars and jets amid so much poverty. Many people in their churches are poor, but the pastors do not care.

According to Britannica.com, Cyrus was born between 590 and 580 BC. Astyages, the king of Medes, gave his daughter in marriage to a prince called Cambyses. The couple was blessed with a boy named Cyrus. Astyages ordered the grandson to be slain for he had a dream that Cyrus had grown up to overthrow him.

The baby was given to a shepherd who raised him. When Cyrus became a man, he formed military gangsters who revolt against his grandfather. Astyages's army deserted him and surrendered to Cyrus in 550 BC. Cyrus became king of the Persians and decided to build his kingdom. He married Cassandane and had six children: Cambyses II, Atossa, Bardya, Roxane, Artystone, and Parmys.

Cyrus decided to expand his territory, and he marched against Lydia. Sardis, the capital of Lydia, was captured in 546 BC. The Greek cities that were vassals to Lydia submitted to Cyrus. Next in line was Babylon. The people of Babylon did not like the leader, Nabonidus, so it was easy for Cyrus to capture this great ancient metropolis in October 539 BC.

According to study.com, one of the major territories conquered by Cyrus was the Babylonian kingdom. The Babylonians captured Jerusalem in 587 BC and forced all the Jewish inhabitants into exile in Babylon. This period was known as the Babylonian captivity. Since Isaiah had already given a prophecy about Cyrus, the Jewish community in Babylon saw him as their liberators. They helped Cyrus's army overthrow the Babylonians.

In 538 BC, Cyrus allowed about forty thousand Jews to returned to Jerusalem, ending the Babylonian captivity. Cyrus used the funds he had acquired in conquering

Babylon to rebuild the sacred temple in Jerusalem, as given in prophecy by Isaiah.

Forty thousand Jews were led by Ezra to rebuild Jerusalem, the temple, so that the Jews would be able to offer sacrifices to their God.

After conquering the Babylonians, Cyrus issued one of the world's first human rights charters. A cylinder containing this charter was discovered during an excavation of ancient Babylon in 1878. In the charter, Cyrus promised to treat all the inhabitants of Babylon and other kingdoms he conquered with respect. He swore that he would allow all inhabitants of his empire to practice their own religious and social customs without persecution. Cyrus also promised to punish anyone who acted cruelly to the religious and social minorities of his kingdom.

Cyrus forbade the seizure of farmers' lands and properties and made slavery of any kind illegal. Cyrus's commitment to fair and equitable treatment of his people is exemplary by modern standards and was unique during his time. Aside from the Cyrus cylinder, there is also the "Edict of Cyrus," which was a written proclamation that authorized and encouraged the Jews exiled by Nebuchadnezzar to return home and rebuild the temple and Jerusalem.

In the ancient Near Eastern thought, there had been a struggle to settle the reason why humans were created:

> Sumerian and Akkadian sources consistently portray people as having been created to do the work of the gods—work that is essential for the continuing existence of the gods, and work that they have tired of doing for themselves. In Israel people also believed that they had been created to serve God.

> The difference is that they saw humanity as having been given a priestly role in sacred space rather than as slave labor to meet the needs of deity. God planted garden to provide food for people rather than people providing foods for the gods.[2]

The Jewish community believes that people are created in the image of God. Human identity is in God and not in any other thing, like riches and wealth. It is not being famous or popular or achieving all the knowledge in this world that make us who we are. It is knowing that we are created in the image of God and that God's purpose for us in this life is to worship and serve Him.

> Even every one that is called by my name; for I have created him for my glory, I have formed him; yea, I have made him. (Isaiah 43:7)

The main reason why God created us is to give Him glory or worship and obey him. God cautioned the Israelites to serve and obey him or suffer for their disobedience. Deuteronomy 28 has sixty-eight verses; the first fourteen verses are blessings that would be on the Israelites if they obeyed God, and the remaining fifty-four verses are curses that would be on the Israelites if they disobeyed God.

> And it shall come to pass, if thou shalt hearken diligently unto the voice of the Lord thy God, to observe and to do all

---

[2] Walton John H., *Ancient Near Eastern Thought and the Old Testament*, Baker Academic Grand Rapids, Michigan, 214.

his commandments which I command thee this day, that the Lord thy God will set thee on high above all nations of the earth: And all these blessings shall come on thee, and overtake thee, if thou shalt hearken unto the voice of the Lord thy God. Blessed shall thou be in the city, and blessed shalt thou be in the field. Blessed shalt be the fruit of thy body, and the fruit of thy ground, and the fruit of thy cattle, the increase of thy kine, and the flocks of thy sheep. Blessed shall be thy basket and thy store. Blessed shalt thou be when thou comest in, and blessed shalt thou be when thou goest out. The Lord shall cause thine enemies that rise up against thee to be smitten before thy face: they shall come out against thee one way, and flee before thee seven ways. The Lord shall command the blessing upon thee in thy store houses, and in all thou settest thine hand unto, and he shall bless thee in the land which the Lord thy God giveth thee: The Lord shall establish thee an holy people unto himself, as he hath sworn unto thee, if thou shalt keep the commandments of the Lord thy God, and walk in his ways. And all the people in the earth shall see that thou art called by the name of the Lord; and they shall be afraid of thee. And the Lord shall make thee plenteous in goods, in the fruit of thy body, and in the fruit of thy cattle, and in the fruit of thy ground, in

> the land which the Lord sware unto thy
> fathers to give thee. The Lord shall open
> unto thee his good treasure, the heaven to
> give the rain unto thy land in his season,
> and to bless all the work of thine hand:
> and thou shalt lend to many nations, and
> thou shalt not borrow. And the Lord shall
> make thee the head, and not the tail: and
> thou shalt be above only, and thou shalt
> not be beneath; if that thou hearken unto
> the commandments of the Lord thy God,
> which I command thee this day, to observe
> and to do them. (Deuteronomy 28:1–14)

The curses start in verse 15 and continue until verse 68. Looking at these blessings might make people think the Israelites would never disobey God. However, we are human. The Israelites disobeyed God several times and went into captivity.

As Christians, we should take note that God is not a man who would lie. We have to take the Word of God seriously and obey the Word of God. The power of God will work on our behalves to see us through this present life. During the reign of Zedekiah, the last king of Judah, Jeremiah, gave a prophecy that the Israelites would be in captivity for seventy years.

> Therefore thus saith the Lord of hosts;
> Because ye have not heard my words,
> Behold I will send and take all the
> families of the north, saith the Lord, and
> Nebuchadnezzar the king of Babylon, my
> servant, and will bring them against this

land, and against the inhabitants thereof, and against all these nations round about, and will utterly destroy them, and make them an astonishment, and a hissing, and perpetual desolations. Moreover I will take from them the voice of mirth, and the voice of gladness, the voice of the bridegroom, and the voice of the bride, the sound of the millstones, and the light of the candle. And this whole land shall be a desolation, and astonishment; and these nations shall serve the king of Babylon seventy years. (Jeremiah 25:8–11)

It is a serious thing to fall into the hands of God. If you disobey him, there is a penalty to pay. For disobeying God, God gave the Israelites over to be slaves of King Nebuchadnezzar. The Israelites were going to serve in Babylon for seventy years.

In Babylon, the Jews were required to sing a song of Zion to their captors.

By the rivers of Babylon, there we sat down, yea, we wept, when we remember Zion. We hanged our harps upon the willows in the midst thereof. For there they that carried us away captive required of a song; and they that wasted us required of us mirth, saying Sing us one of the songs of Zion. How shall we sing the Lord's song in a strange land? If I forget thee O Jerusalem, let my right hand forget her cunning. If I do not remember thee, let my tongue cleave

> to the roof of my mouth; if I prefer not
> Jerusalem above my chief joy. Remember
> O Lord the children of Edom in the day of
> Jerusalem; who said, Rase it, rase it, even
> to the foundation thereof. O daughter of
> Babylon who art to be destroyed; happy
> shall it be, that rewardeth thee as thou
> hast served us. Happy shall he be, that
> taketh and dasheth thy little ones against
> the stone. (Psalm 137:1–9)

The Israelites were going to lose their joy, their children would not marry, and they would not see prosperity. The light of the candle would be taken away. The Israelites were going to walk in spiritual darkness.

According to Psalm 137, the Israelites would never forget Zion, the city of David. The psalm was a plea to the God of Abraham to remember the Jews again. God answered their plea when King Cyrus came up. Many so-called Christians are walking in spiritual darkness, but they are not aware because Satan blindfolded them.

We need to read the Word of God and live a life worthy of emulation, a life according to the Word of God. God found it difficult to do away with the Israelites, and there was another prophecy that Cyrus would deliver them from the hands of the Babylonians after seventy years. The prophecy came in before Cyrus was born.

> Thus saith the Lord to his anointed, to Cyrus,
> whose right hand I have holden, to subdue
> nations before him; and I will lose the loins
> of kings, to open before him the two leaved
> gates; and the gates shall not be shut; I will

go before thee, and make the crooked places straight: I will break in pieces the gates of brass and cut in sunder the bars of iron: And I will give thee the treasures of darkness, and hidden riches of secret places, that thou mayest know that I, the Lord, which call thee by thy name, am the God of Israel. For Jacob my servant's sake and Israel my elect, I have even called thee by thy name: I have surnamed thee, though thou hast not known me. (Isaiah 45:1–4)

Looking at this prophecy, God anointed Cyrus for the job ahead of him. When God calls you, He anoints you with the Holy Spirit so that you can accomplish the purpose of God or the task that is ahead of you. The task ahead of Cyrus was conquering nations and bringing kings into subjection. God was going to lose the loins of kings before Cyrus, which means no king would be able to stand Cyrus. I will open the two leaved gates before Cyrus.

During those days, cities were built with walls and big brass or iron gates. During Cyrus's invasion of Babylon, the priests of Madruk opened the brass gate. God was going to give Cyrus the treasure of darkness and hidden riches from secret places. When God calls you, He will provide what you need for the calling. Cyrus would need finances to build such a great kingdom and rebuild Jerusalem and the temple.

God provided the needed finances for Cyrus. The children of Israel knew they were going into captivity for seventy years. After that, Cyrus—who was not yet born—would become king and deliver them out of the hands of the Babylonians. They did not know how it was going to happen, but God—through Isaiah—said it would be fulfilled.

> God chose Cyrus, the king of Persia, to overwhelm kings, subdue nations and free Israel from their Babylonian oppressors. (On October 29, 539 BC, the priests of Madruk opened the gates of Babylon to the conqueror, and the city capitulated without raising a weapon). Moreover, God's objectives for selecting Cyrus are threefold: personal—that he will come to know the God of Israel; national—for the sake of Israel; and universal—to be the means whereby the entire world will acknowledge God's uniqueness.[3]

Cyrus the Great, affectionately called Father, was kind and faithful to his promises. According to Isaiah's prophecy, God raise him to conquer nations and liberate the Israelites from Babylonian domination.

Looking at most of Cyrus's conquest, it seemed like some unseen force was at the forefront of the battle. It was easy for him to become the king of the Persians. His grandfather, the king of Medes, could not stand Cyrus because his army deserted him and surrendered to Cyrus.

Croesus, the king of Lydia, was afraid when he heard what Cyrus had done to Astyages, the king of Medea. Cyrus easily took over Lydia, treated Croesus very well, and became his partner in other battles. There are so many

---

[3] Paul, Shalom M., *Eerdmans Critical Commentary*; Wm. B. Eerdmans Publishing Co. Grand Rapids, Michigan, 251.

accounts of how Cyrus conquered Babylon. Cyrus set the Israelites free as the prophecy of Isaiah indicated.

The opening book of Ezra gave an account of how Cyrus set the Israelites free:

> Now in the first year of Cyrus king of Persia, that the word of the Lord by the mouth of Jeremiah (that is Israel will be in captivity for seventy years) might be fulfilled, the Lord stirred up the spirit of Cyrus king of Persia, that he made a proclamation throughout all his kingdom, and put it also in writing, saying, Thus saith Cyrus king of Persia, The Lord God of heaven hath given me all the kingdoms of the earth;, and he hath charged me to build him an house at Jerusalem, which is in Judah. Who is there among you of all his people? His God be with him, and let him go up to Jerusalem, which is in Judah, and build the house of the Lord God of Israel, (he is the God,) which is in Jerusalem. And whosoever remaineth in any place where he sojourneth, let the men of his place help him with silver, and with gold, and with goods, and with beasts, beside the freewill offering for the house of God that is in Jerusalem. (Ezra 1:1–4)

This proclamation gave the Israelites the freedom to leave Babylon without being intimidated. Coming out of captivity, the Israelites were blessed with gold, silver, brass, and sheep or goats to help them to do the work of God when they were in Jerusalem.

Cyrus gave the Israelites the vessels of the house of the Lord, which Nebuchadnezzar brought from Jerusalem when he took the Jews captive. Cyrus gave treasures to the house of the Lord in Jerusalem. God inspired Cyrus to commission the Jewish leaders to carry out a threefold mission: rebuild the temple and the city, purify the Jewish community, and seal the holy city with walls.

The first mission was set forth with the Levites. The leader was Zerubbabel, the son of Shealtiel. He was supported by Jeshua, the son of Jozadak. When the foundation of the temple was laid, there was a great joy in Israel. However, the enemies of progress stood against the building of the temple and the great city.

Cyrus the Great was dead, and the Israelites could not complete the building of the temple until the reign of Darius of Persia.

During the reign of Artaxerxes, Bishlam, Mithredath, Tabeel, and their evil friends wrote letters to the king of Persia. Rehum the chancellor and Shimshai the writer wrote letters against Jerusalem to Artaxerxes, the king of Persia, saying the Jews had rebelled against the king by rebuilding Jerusalem and the temple.

The enemies of progress wrote a compelling letter during the reign of Darius. It said that Darius had to see if Cyrus allowed the Jews to rebuild the temple. An edit on a roll showed that King Cyrus had given permission to the Jews to return and rebuild the temple and Jerusalem. The treasures and vessels that were taken by Nebuchadnezzar had been restored to the Jews to be used in the house of God. King Darius told the enemies to leave the Jews alone as they rebuilt the temple and the city.

President Donald Trump declared Jerusalem the capital of Israel, and I hope any president that comes after him will continue the good work. I challenge President Donald Trump not to give in to external or international pressure about building the United States embassy in Jerusalem.

When the embassy is built in Jerusalem, President Donald Trump will see the blessings of God. If he changes his uncouth attitude, accepts Jesus Christ as his Savior, reads the Word of God, abides by the Word, changes his attitude and the way he speaks and hurts the feelings of people, then he may win the next election and be president for eight years.

Due to obstruction and difficulties, the Jews stopped rebuilding of the temple and started building panel houses for themselves and their families. They neglected the most important thing: the temple of God.

During the second year of King Darius, Haggai gave a prophecy that the Jews had abandoned the house of God and built their own houses. That was why they saw no prosperity. Until they changed their ways, they would not see the glory of God.

> Then came the word of the Lord by Haggai the prophet, saying, It is time for you, O ye, to dwell in your ceiled houses, and this house lie waste? Now therefore thus saith the Lord of hosts; Consider your ways. Ye have sown much, and bring in little; ye eat, but ye have not enough; ye drink, but ye are not filled with drink; ye cloth you, but there is none warm, and he that earneth wages earneth wages to put it into a bag with holes. Thus saith the Lord of hosts; Consider your

> ways. Go up to the mountain, and bring
> wood, and build the house; and I will take
> pleasure in it, and I will be glorified, saith
> the Lord. (Haggai 1:3–8)

When God spoke through Haggai, Zerubbabel—the governor of Judah and Josedech—the high priest, and the rest of the people came together to build the house of the Lord. They were strengthened by the Word of God from the prophets. The glory of the new house would be greater than the former one. Since God was with them, they should not be afraid of what their enemies would do. They persisted and built the temple.

The Jews had to consider their ways because they had left the work of God to do their own work. The enemies were working hard against them. Instead of trusting in God to see them through, they gave in to their enemies. They left the building of the temple, and God said they worked so much but saw few results. Even when they ate, they were never full. They earned money to be put in a bag full of holes. This is spiritual and deep. Many so-called Christians are earning the almighty dollar, but they put it in a bag full of holes. Many Christians have neglected the Word of God, and the work of God means nothing to them. They earn a lot of money, but they do not know why the money flies away from them.

In Ghana, people say, "Money has wings to fly." If you do not abide by the Word of God, the funds will fly away from you. Until they reconsider and change their ways of life, they will never see prosperity. When God showed the Jews what to do to change their situation—go to the mountain and get wood to build the temple—they finally listened to Him.

Zechariah gave an encouraging prophecy that helped Zerubbabel finish building the house of the Lord.

> Then he answered and spake unto me, saying, This is the word of the Lord unto Zerubbabel, saying, Not by might, nor by power, but by my spirit, saith the Lord of hosts. Who art thou, O great mountain? Before Zerubbabel thou shalt become a plain: and he shall bring forth the headstone thereof with shoutings, crying, Grace, unto it. Moreover the word of the Lord came to me, saying, The hands of Zerubbabel have laid the foundation of this house; his hands shall also finish it; and thou shalt know that the Lord of host sent me unto you. (Zechariah 4:6–9)

The prophets of God played an important role in building the temple. They received encouraging messages from God. The might, the intelligence, the strength, and the technical know-how of the Israelites would not build the temple. The Spirit of God would build the temple.

If you are a child of God and commit your ways to God, then God will show you what project to tackle. When you start, your spiritual enemies will not prosper. The Spirit of God will start and finish the project.

The "great mountain" refers to the enemies of progress, and it will become plain. I pray to the Spirit of God that any mountain before President Donald Trump will become plain for him so he can fulfill his promise of building the American embassy in Jerusalem. Holy Spirit, I pray that you will give President Donald Trump the wisdom granted to King Solomon to rule America and build the American embassy soon in Jerusalem. The world will know that you, God, are still on your throne. The mountain before Zerubbabel was crushed and became plain. In the same way, God, please crush the enemies of President Donald Trump and let them become plain. In the name of Jesus Christ, your beloved Son. Amen!

The second mission of King Cyrus was to purify the Jewish community. That was the major work of the high priest and his Levite priests. The high priest was Jeshua, the son of Jozadok. Jeshua contributed to the purification process and helped Zerubbabel build the temple. They needed an altar to offer sacrifices to the Lord, so Jeshua and his brothers—the Levites—helped build an altar in the new temple.

> Then stood up Jeshua the son of Jozadak, and his brethren the priests, and Zerubbabel the son of Shealtiel, and his brethren, and builded the altar of the God of Israel, to offer burnt offering thereon, as it is written in the law of Moses the man of God. And they set the altar upon his bases; for fear was upon them because of the people of those countries: and they offered burnt offerings morning and evening. They kept also the feast of the tabernacles, as it is written, and offered the daily burnt offerings by number, according the custom, as the duty of every day required; And afterwards offered the continual burnt offering, both of the new moons, and all the set feasts of the Lord

that were consecrated, and of every one
that willingly offered a freewill offering
unto the Lord. (Ezra 3:2–5)

The high priest and his brothers—the Levites—started teaching the people the Word of God as given through Moses. They were afraid, but they did not stop the work of God. They were afraid of the enemies of progress. Even though they were afraid, they did not stop the work of God.

President Donald Trump, do not stop the work of God even though you may be afraid. I pray that God will strengthen you with the Holy Spirit to be bold even in the face of the enemies of progress. The high priest and the Levites offered the burned offering and other sacrifices to God, and they kept the feasts of the tabernacles and Passover. The Levites did well in teaching the people to abide by the Word of God so that they would see good health, well-being, and prosperity.

The third mission was to secure the borders of Jerusalem, and this was accomplished by Nehemiah. It was easy to travel between Jerusalem and Babylon when some of the Jews returned home after the captivity. Some men came to Babylon. Nehemiah's brother told him that the walls of Jerusalem were broken down and the gates had been burned with fire.

The Jews were afflicted, and it was not easy to come back from captivity to start life anew. Nehemiah became so sad while he was serving the king in the palace.

King Artaxerxes noticed his countenance and asked Nehemiah why he was so sad.

Nehemiah prayed to God to find favor in the sight of the king, and God granted him that favor. Nehemiah told the king that Jerusalem's walls were broken down, the

gates had been burned, and the city had been laid to waste. "When will you come if you go and build it?"

Nehemiah gave the king a set time, and the king gave him permission to build the walls of Jerusalem. Nehemiah asked for letters from the king to the governors and Asaph, the keeper of the king's forest, so that Nehemiah would be able to get timber to make beams for the gates of the palace, which was attached to the wall.

When Cyrus died, his children fought about who would ascend to the throne.

> He [Cyrus] ... did not know, however, that his intended heirs were not being instructed in the traditional Persian discipline. This discipline (the Persian being shepherds, and sons of a stony soil) was a tough one, capable of producing hardy shepherds who could camp out and keep awake on watch and turn soldier if necessary. He just didn't notice that women and eunuchs had given his sons the education of a Mede, and that it had been debased by their so-called 'blessed' status. That is why Cyrus' children turned out as children naturally do when their teachers have never corrected them. So when they succeeded to their inheritance on the death of Cyrus, they lived in a riot of unrestrained debauchery. First, unwilling to tolerate an equal, one of them killed the other.[4]

---

[4] Wiesehofer, *Josef Ancient Persia*; I. B. Tauris Publishers, New York, NY, 79.

If you are a king, a president, or a CEO who neglects your house, your children will grow up to be wayward. David was so immersed in wars that he forgot his fatherly duties. His kids became wayward, and Absalom stood against David to take his throne from him. I pray that pastors, Christian CEOs, and presidents will not neglect their fatherly duties because the enemy will turn their houses into war zones.

The infighting of who should ascend to the throne brought King Artaxerxes to the throne. King Artaxerxes was the fifth king of Persia from 465 BC to 424 BC. He was the grandson of King Darius.

The decree issued by King Cyrus—who was dead and gone—was still working wonders for the Jews. During the reign of Darius, Cyrus's edict revealed that King Cyrus had set the Israelites free to rebuild the temple. King Darius allowed the Jews to continue with the work.

Since the grandson of Darius, King Artaxerxes, knew the history of the Jewish people, it was easier for him to grant Nehemiah permission to rebuild the walls:

> And it come to pass in the month Nisan, in the twentieth year of Artaxerxes, the king, that wine was before him: and I took up the wine, and gave it unto the king. Now I had not been beforetime sad in his presence, Wherefore the king said unto me, Why is thy countenance sad, seeing thou art not sick? This is nothing else but sorrow of heart. Then I was very sore afraid, And said unto the king, Let the king live for ever: why should not my countenance be sad, when the city, the place of my fathers' sepulchers, lieth waste, and the gates

thereof are consumed with fire? Then the king said unto me, For what dost thou make request? So I prayed to the God of heaven. And I said unto the king, if it pleased the king, and if thy servant have found favor in thy sight, that thou wouldest send me unto Judah, unto the city of my fathers' sepulchers, that I may build it. And the king said unto me, (the queen also sitting by him,) For how long shall thy journey be? And when will thou return? So it pleased the king to send me; and I set him a time. Moreover I said unto the king, If it please the king, let letters be given me to the governors beyond the rivers, that they may convey me over till I come to Judah; And a letter unto Asaph the keeper of the king's forest, that he may give me timber to make beams for the gates of the palace which appertained to the house, and for the wall of the city, and for the house which I shall enter into. And the king granted me, according to the good hand of my God upon me. (Nehemiah 2:1–8)

Nehemiah was able to get a passage through to Jerusalem because of the letters he received from King Artaxerxes. When Sanballat the Horonite and Tobiah the Ammonite heard that someone had come to Jerusalem to check on the welfare of the Jews, they were furious.

Nehemiah did not care what the enemies did or said. He trusted God to see him through with the project. President Donald Trump, do not be afraid of present-day

Tobiahs and Sanballats. They cannot do anything to you. The Lord is on your side. I wish I was an American citizen. I would be voting for you in the next election because of your bold action.

When Nehemiah got to Jerusalem, he spent three days surveying the walls and seeing what could be done. He did not tell anyone what his mission was until he finished his reconnaissance. Many Christians have "okro mouth," which means they cannot keep anything to themselves. In Ghana, having okro mouth means you cannot be trusted because you cannot keep a secret. People with okro mouth will spill out any vision or dream God has given them. Be careful. Not everyone has your best interests at heart.

After Joseph's brothers sold him into slavery, God turned Joseph's misery into the deliverance of Israel. Nehemiah did not just walk around; he was also praying to God. After three days, Nehemiah told the people about his mission. The people were in full support. He told them about building the walls of Jerusalem and how the hand of God had been the leading role in this project. The people were so excited and started building the walls.

Eliashib, the high priest, and his brothers started by building the sheep gate and sanctifying it. It gave the rest of the people the energy to work. The families worked on the walls. Shallum, the son of Halohesh and ruler of half of Jerusalem, came with his daughters to work on the wall.

While the Jewish people were busy building the wall, the enemies of progress—Sanballat, Tobiah, and Geshem— laughed them to scorn and asked if they would rebel against the king. Nehemiah said, "The God of heaven, he will prosper us; therefore we his servants will arise and build: but ye have no portion, nor right, nor memorial, in Jerusalem."

There is opposition anytime anyone tries to do the will of God. It can come from family, friends, or coworkers. Do not listen to what others are doing or saying about your good works. You will see good results as you continue to trust in the Lord.

The people worked on the wall as a team. They worked together with one accord and one mind. When Sanballat and Tobiah heard that the wall was being built, they were angry. They conspired to fight against Jerusalem. This conspiracy was made known to Nehemiah, and the Jews called upon God and gathered spears, swords, and bows as they worked on the walls. It got to the point where they had to build with one hand while the other hand held a weapon.

Nehemiah was appointed governor in Jerusalem, and he worked tirelessly for his people. He brought fairness and equity to his administration. The Jews liked him as a leader.

Tobiah and Sanballat never stopped being jerks. When Nehemiah finished building the walls, Tobiah and Sanballat were still finding ways to get rid of Jeremiah. Present-day jerks in the church try to bring down the work of God. I believe God will deal with anyone who is an enemy of progress in the church.

> Now it came to pass, when Sanballat and Tobiah and Geshem, the Arabian, and the rest of our enemies, heard that I had builded the wall, and that there was no breach left therein (though at that time I had not set up the doors upon the gates;) That Sanballat and Geshem sent unto me, saying, Come, let us meet together in some one of the villages in the plain of Ono. But they thought to do me mischief. And I sent messengers unto

them, saying, I am doing a great work, so that I cannot come down: why should the work cease, whilst I leave it, and come down to you? Yet they sent unto me four times after this sort; and I answered them after the same manner. Then sent Sanballat his servant unto me in the like manner the fifth time with an open letter in his hand; Wherein was written, It is reported among the heathen, and Gashmu saith it, that thou and the Jews think to rebel: for which cause thou buildest the wall, that thou mayest be their king, according to these words. And thou hast also appointed prophets to preach to thee at Jerusalem saying, There is a king in Judah: and now shall it be reported to the king according to these words. Come now therefore, and let us take counsel together. Then I sent unto him, saying, There are no such things done as thou sayest, but thou feignest them out of thine own heart. (Nehemiah 6:1–8)

Sanballat said four times that Nehemiah should meet for a talk, but he wanted him dead. The fifth time, Sanballat sent his servant, Tobiah, with an open letter that accused Nehemiah of rebelling against the king. It also claimed Nehemiah was trying to be the king of the Jews—and that was why Nehemiah was building the walls.

The allegations did not bother Nehemiah. He knew they were all false. Nehemiah continued with the work of God instead of listening to fake news or lies. President Donald Trump, do not listen to any fake news. Do your best to accomplish what God has called you to do. Follow your words with action by building the American embassy in Jerusalem.

Sanballat, Tobiah, and Geshum were wicked people who would stop at nothing to achieve their demonic mission. They hired a Jewish prophet to take Nehemiah to the temple.

Nehemiah realized that the prophet was lying to him, and he did not go. As children of God, we should be able to discern when the enemy is working against us. That is a gift of the Holy Spirit, and I wish every child of God will desire it. If Nehemiah did not discern the truth, he would have been dead before his time.

> Afterwards I came unto the house of Shemaiah the son of Delaiah the son of Mehetabell, who was shut up, and he said, Let us meet together in the house of God, within the temple, and let us shut the doors of the temple: for they will come to slay thee; yea, in the night will they come to slay thee. And I said, Should such a man as I flee? And who is there that, being as I am, would go into the temple to save his life? I will not go in. And lo, I perceived that God had not sent him; but that he pronounced this prophecy against me: for Tobiah and Sanballat had hired him. (Nehemiah 6:10–12)

The love of money is the root of all evil. A prophet of God started lying because of money. In Africa, men of God ride in Mercedes-Benzes. Some have jets and live in a million-dollar mansions. Half of their congregation are poor and find it difficult to get three square meals. For the love of money, these ministers have neglected the Word of God and are living exorbitant lives at the expense of their congregations. A bad nut spoils the soup. Not all of them are like that. On the internet, I found a Nigerian minister who has a free school for. The kids are fed through the church coffers. I was pleased when I saw some genuine ministers out there.

Nehemiah was full of wisdom, and he knew which prophecies were from God and which were not. Sanballat tried to scare Nehemiah so that he would stop building the walls of Jerusalem, but nothing could deter this man of God from what God had destined him to be. Fear makes many Christians lose focus and the destiny God ordained for them. Despite the confrontations and opposition of the enemies, Nehemiah was able to finish the walls of Jerusalem in fifty-two days. A lot of prophets tried to scare Nehemiah, including Shemaiah and Noadiah, but Nehemiah did not fall for their dirty tricks. He focused on God and finished the walls.

After the completion of the walls, Nehemiah appointed his brother Hananiah to keep charge over Jerusalem. Hananiah was a faithful man who feared God. Today, many churches appoint leaders without looking at character. They look at how financially sound the person is. Some even pay bribes to be appointed as leaders. Those who can give financial bounty to the church often win the hearts of the leaders.

Nehemiah looked for faithfulness and fear of God. He had been given a divine direction to gather all the nobles and rulers to reckon the people with their genealogy. An important census counted how many Jews came out of the

Babylonian captivity. After the census, the people came together and called Ezra to read the book of the Law of Moses to the whole congregation. The congregation fasted and confessed their sins and the sins of their forefathers to the God of Israel.

Nehemiah had to travel to the palace in Babylon to brief King Artaxerxes on what he had been able to accomplish. The book of Moses said that the Moabites and the Ammonites should not come into the congregation of Israel because they had hired Balaam to curse the Israelites during their exodus to the Promised Land. God turned the curses into blessings.

Tobiah was working wickedly with Sanballat to stop the building of the walls, and Eliashib entertained Tobiah in the house of God. Nehemiah was furious when he came from Babylon to find out, and he threw Tobiah out of the house of God. Nehemiah cautioned the Israelites not to marry strange wives (foreigners). One of the sons of Joiada, the son of Eliashib, was the son-in-law of Sanballat.

Nehemiah brought the wholeness, sanity, and faithfulness of the Jewish community to the God of Israel.

The hand of God moved to set the Israelites free from the Babylonian captivity through the Edict of Cyrus. This fulfilled the prophecy of Isaiah about Cyrus almost two hundred years before Cyrus was born.

In about 538 BC, Ezra led about forty thousand Jews back to their homeland and started rebuilding Jerusalem. Even after the death of Cyrus, the Cyrus Edict helped in the building of the temple. Zerubbabel started and finished the temple.

King Artaxerxes knew about the Cyrus Edict and gave Nehemiah permission to rebuild the walls of Jerusalem. Nehemiah started and finished the walls of Jerusalem.

God used men of God to rebuild Jerusalem after it was burned by Nebuchadnezzar.

Every project you start will be faced with opposition from Satan and his dark forces. I want every Christian who is living according to the Word of God to know that God has not forgotten you. At the right time, you will see the hand of God leveling any mountain before you, making the crooked path straight, and filling up any valley before you. He has called us, and He is faithful. God will surely keep all his promises concerning our lives. The only part we need to play in this Christian life is to abide by the Word of God. We need to live lives that are worthy of our calling. We cannot say we are Christian while living our own lives and conforming to the standard of this world.

I want to warn President Donald Trump that there will be a lot of opposition from Arab countries, the United Nations, Europe, and even Americans. Please look unto God and not at what others are saying. I wish you would stop texting and leave all battles in the hands of God. I know many people are going to rise against this book, but I trust God to get it published. I believe the Holy Spirit will fight any battle in the name of Jesus Christ.

President Donald Trump called African countries "shitholes." Many people were furious, but that was the truth. I am a Ghanaian, and I had the opportunity to be educated in Prempeh College, Kumasi. That was like being educated at Harvard. I also studied mining engineering at the University of Science and Technology School of Mines in Tarkwa, Ghana. I know what I am talking about.

In 1983, John Dickson Baidu and I wrote a report about oil and minerals in Ghana while we were students at the School of Mines. It took the country more than twenty years to realize that Ghana is rich in oil. I became a supervisor at Akwatia Diamond Mines, and John Dickson Baidu worked in the Ventilation Department in Obuasi Gold Mines. I know about the mines in Ghana.

If Ghana is so rich in minerals, why is it among the poorest countries on earth? This is due to corruption and mismanagement. The leaderships of Ghana was so corrupt that Ghana is a shithole country. How can Woyomi be among the richest people in Ghana? It is because of corruption. Ex-president Mahama and his cronies left Ghana in shambles. They stole from the national coffers and left the country in poverty.

Of all the presidents of Ghana, Dr. Kwame Nkrumah was the only one who did not steal from the national coffers. He also made some mistakes by giving away huge sums of money to Guinea and other countries. Many people are rich due to corruption. The police force is one of the most corrupt institutions in the country.

President Nana Akufo-Addo, to be frank, you have inherited a shithole country. I believe you will not steal from the national coffers, but will you do your best to deal with the people who had got their wealth through corruption? President Nana Akufo-Addo, thanks for the free education. I believe God chose you as the president of Ghana. Please do your best to lift Ghana from an underdeveloped country to at least a second world country. Let Ghana be the star of Africa. Let the black star shine. Do your best to follow in the footsteps of President Donald Trump. If you move Ghana's embassy from Tel Aviv to Jerusalem, God will richly bless you.

I saw a Ghanaian burning an American visa because of what President Donald Trump said, but that was foolishness. In the process, he burned the Ghanaian passport, a valuable document. The government has to arrest this foolish person, jail him for five years, and never issue him another Ghanaian passport. This fool could have taken the visa out of the passport and only burned the visa.

> Pray for the peace of Jerusalem: they shall
> prosper that love thee. (Psalm 122:6)

The Bible cautions us to pray for the peace of Jerusalem. Father God, I would like to take this opportunity to pray for the peace of Jerusalem and Israel. Please let the Holy Spirit be a wall of fire surrounding the state of Israel. Father, bless the leadership—Prime Minister Benjamin Netanyahu and Knesset—to issue policies that will favor the citizen. Father, let them not forget that they are the great-great-grandchildren of Abraham, and your hand is upon their nation. Father God, bless Jerusalem and Israel in the name of Jesus. Amen.

Anyone who loves Jerusalem is going to prosper. I hope President Nana Akufo-Addo loves Jerusalem and moves the Ghanaian embassy from Tel Aviv to Jerusalem. When you do that, God has promised to help you prosper.

The high-speed train that Dr. Thomas wants to bring to Ghana is a good idea. Please exercise and take good care of yourself. Ghana needs you. I have been praying for you, and I believe all your enemies who come against you in one way will flee in seven other ways. God will fight your battles for you.

The Philistines who came against the Israelites in the time of Samuel were destroyed by thunder and lightning, and anyone who comes against Nana Akufo-Addo will be destroyed by thunder and lightning. Mr. President, stay in the Lord Jesus Christ and be in shape. May the Lord richly bless you and your family.

President Akufo-Addo, I loved what you said at the Third International Conference on the Replenishment of the Funds of the Global Partnership for Education in Dakar, Senegal. You said, "There is an abundance of resources on the continent to finance the development of Africa, and the resources can be put to good use by eliminating corruption in public life."

You have hit the bull's-eye. Corruption and mismanagement is keeping Africa underdeveloped. Even Rihanna said that Ghanaians ought to be proud to have a head of state like President Nana Addo Dankwa Akufo-Addo. The president shook hands with Rihanna at the International Education Summit in Dakar. Nana, we trust you. We believe you will turn around the economy and do away with corruption in Ghana. I hope you are going to be a man of your word and bring integrity into the politics of Ghana. May the Lord bless you.

I will be very grateful if you move the Ghanaian embassy from Tel Aviv to Jerusalem. Look at the Word of God. He has placed His name in Jerusalem. Please do not think of what other nations or people are going to say and act according to the Word of God. I am really amazed when I hear you speak, and I hope you will back your words with action.

The speech you delivered at the Kukah Centre in Nigeria on February 16, 2018, was marvelous. According to ghanaweb.com:

> President Nana Addo Dankwa Akufo-Addo has challenged his colleague African leaders to make the continent attractive for the youth. That, he explained, would make them see the continent as a place

of opportunities. He bemoaned the fact that African youth "brave the Sahara Desert on foot, and those who survive the ravages of the desert risk being sold on slave markets in Libya or risk journeys across the Mediterranean Sea on rickety boats, all in the forlorn hope of better life in Europe, in countries and among people where they are obviously not welcome."

If there is no reformation or transformation of governments in Africa, then Africa will never see development and prosperity. The youth are going to be affected, and they will find ways—fair or foul—to get out. Delivering the keynote address at a conference on transformative governance in Africa in Abuja, Nigeria, President Akuffo-Addo said, "Our youth who bear the burnt of suffering who now resort to desperate measures to get out."

Can someone tell me why almost every country in the world hates Israel? Israel will prosper and will be like a palm tree. God will never leave or forsake Israel.

The literacy rate in Israel is amazing: total population: 97.8 percent, male: 98.7 percent, and female: 96.8 percent. The colleges and universities in Israel are among the best in the world.

The literacy rate Ghana needs to improve: total population: 76.6 percent, male: 82 percent, and female: 71.4 percent.

Thanks, President Nana Akufo-Addo, for the free education system. I believe the literacy rate in Ghana will be higher in about five years. Nana, do your best to be a friend of Israel and build a good foreign relationship with Israel. God will bless you. The Ghanaians trusted and voted you into power. Do your best not to disappoint the masses. I trust that the good hand of the Lord Jesus will be on you to give you wisdom and strength to rule Ghana, the beacon of Africa.

After seventy years, the tiny nation of Israel is among the leading edge in technology and has been named "the start-up nation." On November 17, 2017, Israel returned to the hall in Flushing Meadows, New York, where the crucial vote to establish a Jewish state was held on November 29, 1947. Israel's mission to the United Nations celebrated the seventieth anniversary of the historic United Nations vote on Resolution 181 that called for the establishment of a Jewish state. The event took place at the Queens Museum, which served as UN headquarters in 1947. Vice President Mike Pence was the guest of honor and delivered the keynote address on the eve of his planned visit to Israel.

2

THE MODERN-DAY
ISRAEL (PART A)

-Zion is a hill in Jerusalem on which the city of David was built. Thus, Zion and Jerusalem are interchangeable.

> For Zion's sake will I not hold my peace,
> and for Jerusalem's sake I will not rest,
> until the righteousness thereof go forth as
> brightness, and thy salvation thereof as a
> lamp that burneth. And the Gentiles shall
> see thy righteousness, and all kings thy
> glory; and thou shalt be called a new name,
> which the mouth of the Lord shall name.
> (Isaiah 62:1–2)

This is the promise of God to Israel that He is not going to hold his peace or rest till this nation is fully established.

The migration of the Jews started around the fourth century BC. Sephardic Jewish settlement occurred in the Aegean region, and Jewish settlements occurred in Anatolia. Josephus Flavius said that Aristotle met some Jewish people and exchanged views with them during his trip across Asia Minor. In the Asia Minor region, ancient synagogue ruins had been located in Sardis dating as far back as 220 BC.

Emperor Augustus gave the right accorded for the

Jewish settlements in the Asia Minor. Jewish communities had been thriving in Anatolia even before the Turkish conquest. In 1324, the Ottomans conquered Bursa and made it a capital. They found a Jewish settlement that had been oppressed under the Byzantine rule.

Many Jews migrated from Europe to Edirne in the fourteenth century when the Ottomans made Edirne their capital. Jews were expelled from Hungary in 1376, from France in September 1394 by Charles VI, and from Sicily in early fifteenth century. The Jews quickly sought refuge in the Ottoman Empire.

Several Jews who were persecuted in other parts of Europe sought refuge in the Ottoman Empire. Constantinople was taken over by Sultan Mehmet II, and he was welcome by the Jews in Romaniote (Byzantine). In 1470, the Jews who were kicked out of Bavaria by Ludwig X sought refuge in the Ottoman Empire. The Jews were expelled from Spain in 1492 by Isabelle I and Ferdinand II, which brought hardship to thousands of Jews. The Ottoman Empire became a safe haven for the Jews. The Jews were kicked out of Italy in 1537 and from Bohemia by King Ferdinand in 1542. They found comfort in the Ottoman Empire. The Jews in the Ottoman Empire became so prosperous, and four Turkish cities—Istanbul, Izmir, Safed, and Salonika—became centers of Sephardic Jewry. One of the most important innovations that the Jews brought to the Ottoman Empire was the printing press. David and Samuel Ibn Nahmias started the first Hebrew printing press in Istanbul after they were expelled from Spain.

Since the time of the Ottoman Empire, the desire of the Jews to return to the homeland has been debated. Many thought it was not feasible since the Ottoman Empire was against the immigration of Jews and their settlement in the Promised Land. The Promised Land in Palestine was occupied by more than half a million Arabs.

Zion is in Jerusalem, and to the Jews, Zion stands for the Promised Land. Therefore, Zionism is a movement of Jews in the Diaspora who had the desire to return to the Promised Land.

The Jewish Diaspora refers to Jewish communities living outside of Israel.

> The Zionist movement was born amid stormy controversy that attends it to this day, although the focus of contention varies. What was Zionism, anyway? A renaissance movement directed toward reshaping the Jews, Jewish society, Jewish culture? A colonization movement aiming to establish a Jewish territorial entity that would grant the Jews what other peoples had: a homeland where they could find refuge? A spiritual or political movement? Could Zionism resolve the question of Jewish identity in the era of rising secularization and acculturation, with religion no longer able to save the Jews from atomization? Could it relieve the Jewish existential anxiety that had been on the rise since the last quarter of the nineteenth century, when a racism-oriented anti-Semitism emerged that for the first time in history refused Jews the option of conversion as an escape from the Jewish fate? These questions, which

attended the internal Zionist disputes from the beginning and were posed by the movement's own adherents, bore fateful implications for Zionism's character and development, its strengths and weakness.[5]

Simply put, Zionism is the national movement of Jewish people who support the creation of a Jewish homeland in the territory considered to be the historic land of Israel. Theodor Herzl was the founder of *Modern Zionist*, and he had a vision of a future independent Jewish state during the twentieth century. He wrote *Der Judenstaat* in 1896 and suggested the establishment of the state of Israel in the twentieth century.

The Jewish people were dispersed throughout Western and Eastern Europe and Russia. These Jews were stuck in Jewish culture, customs, and traditions that could not match the industrialization and modernization that were turning Europe upside down. It was difficult for the Jews to study the language of the people and go to school with the natives, which left most of the Jews in poverty. The Jews of the Western Europe were able to integrate and assimilate; therefore, a large proportion of the young Zionist movement leaders was from the West.

In contrast, the masses that Zionism sought to save lived in Eastern Europe and knew little of Western culture. Many remained immersed in a religious lifestyle and observed the Halakha (Jewish law) and tradition. The accelerated modernization

---

[5] Anita Shapira, *Israel: A History*; Brandeis University Press, Waltham, Massachusetts; 3.

in the Tsarist Empire in the second half of the nineteenth century and the early twentieth affected broad strata of this population: the railways made the Jewish peddler redundant, traditional occupations such as carting became unnecessary, and numerous crafts lost their economic role in the wake of industrialization. The lost of these sources of livelihood, combined with population increase among the Jews of Tsarist Russia between 1840 and 1900, led to wide scale poverty. The preferred solution of economic hardship, an absence of physical security, and lack of hope was emigration overseas. At the turn of the century, immigration to the United States seemed to be the solution for millions of distressed Jews, but even though many left for the New World, on the eve of World War One the number of Jews in the Russia Empire had actually increased from 1882.[6]

In between the World War I and World War II, the number of Jews in Europe increased dramatically. There were about nine million Jews living in Europe, both the West and East, when the Nazis came to power in 1933. Almost every country where the Jews lived was occupied by the Nazis during World War II, and by the end of this war, about two-thirds of Jews were dead.

Before 1993, the largest Jewish population in Europe was concentrated in Poland, the Soviet Union, Hungary,

---

[6] Anita Shapira, *Israel: A History*, University Press Brandeis, Waltham, Massachusetts; 20.

and Romania. It was easy to identify these Jews in Eastern Europe because they lived in their own minority settlements, which were known as shtetls. They did not learn the native language and spoke Yiddish, which was a combination of German and Hebrew. They had their own schools to teach Jewish traditions and culture. The older people dressed traditionally. The men wore caps or hats, and the women traditionally covered their heads with wigs or kerchiefs.

The young people did their best to adapt to the people they lived with. The Jews in Germany, France, the Netherlands, Italy, and Belgium tended to adapt to the culture of their native countryman and think less about Jewish religious and Yiddish culture. They dressed and talked like the countrymen and were in the same schools. Jews could be found in every area of business; they were farmers, factory hands, tailors, seamstresses, doctors, accountants, teachers, and small business owners. Few Jewish families were wealthy, and the majority were poor. The young ones were educated, and some went to universities, but with the rise of the Nazis in Germany, every Jew was a potential victim of victimization and death.

Poland was occupied by the Germans, and it was the final doom of the Jews. About three million Jews were killed in Poland. There were death camps in Belzec, Sobibor, and Treblinka. Gas chambers were constructed at Majdanek and Auschwitz for the "final solution of the Jewish question." The genocide was officially sanctioned and executed by the Third Reich during World War II. The Holocaust took the lives of more than three million Polish Jews.

Mateusz Morawiecki, the Polish prime minister, said, "There were some Jews perpetrators." I think he should give an apology to Israel because the Jews were victims in the Holocaust and not perpetrators. According to politico. eu, Israeli Prime Minister Benjamin Netanyahu called the comments "outrageous" and showed an inability to understand history.

Morawiecki made the comments at the Munich Security Conference, which took place on February 16–18, 2018) to answer a question from an Israeli journalist about a new Polish law that made it illegal to accuse Poland of complicity in Nazi crimes. He said, "It's extremely important to first understand that of course it is not going to be punishable, not going to be seen as criminal to say that there were Polish perpetrators—as there were there were Jewish perpetrators, as there were Russian perpetrators, as there were Ukrainian—not only German perpetrators."

Netanyahu said, "The Polish prime minister's remarks here in Munich are outrageous. There is a problem here of inability to understand history and a lack of sensitivity to the tragedy of our people."

I learned about World War II and how the Nazis and their allies killed more than six million Jews in Europe. Three million of them were Polish. How could the Jews have been the perpetrators? I think the Polish prime minister needs a history lesson.

Jewish in Europe should never forget important dates. In September 1791, the French National Assembly declared the emancipation of the Jews, which meant the Jews would be granted citizenship if they took a loyalty oath. This was later followed by Greece in 1830, Great Britain in 1858, Italy in 1870, Germany in 1871, and Norway in 1891. The Jews still had to live with anti-Semitism and social discrimination.

On June 24, 1922, a Jewish politician was assassinated in Germany. Walter Rathenau was the president of General

Electric Corporation of Germany. He became the foreign minister of the Weimar Republic and was assassinated for his policy of fulfilling the terms of the Treaty of Versailles and normalization of relations with Soviet Union. He was an important political figure.

On March 9, 1936, violence erupted in Poland. More than sixty Jews were killed in a pogrom in the city of Przytyk. The pogroms throughout Europe killed more than two hundred Jews. A pogrom is an organized massacre or persecution of Jews.

Life for Jews in Europe during the Second World War was dreadful and scary. It was estimated that nine million Jews lived in Europe just before World War II. About six million Jews died in the Holocaust. The current Jewish population in Europe is around 2.4 million:

- Ashkenazi Jews (about 1.4 million living in France, Germany, Russia, Ukraine, the United Kingdom, Hungary, and Belgium)
- Sephardic Jews (nearly 400,000 in France, Turkey, Greece, Bulgaria, and Bosnia and Herzegovina)
- Mizrahi Jews (around 300,000 in France, Spain, Georgia, the United Kingdom, and Azerbaijan)
- Turkish Jews (around 250,000 known as Djudios Turkos, minorities of about 20,000 Selanikis and 25,000 Sephardics)
- Italian Jews (about 45,000 in Italy)
- Romaniotes (about 6,000 in Greek)
- Georgian Jews (around 8,500 in Georgia, Russia, Azerbaijan, and Belgium)
- Crimean Karaites (around 1,500 in Ukraine, Lithuania, and Poland)

- Krymchaks (of Turkic descent in Crimea) (about 2,000 mainly in Ukraine, Azerbaijan, Georgia, and Russia)
- Mountain Jews (Jews of the Caucasus found in Azerbaijan)

The Holocaust, which is also referred to as the Shoah, was the genocide, destruction, and slaughter of European Jews during the Second World War. Adolf Hitler's Nazis and collaborators murdered about six million Jews in Europe. The SS, with direction from the highest leadership of the Nazi Party, passed a law to exclude Jews from civil society, the Nuremberg Laws in 1935. The Nazis started building concentration camps in Germany for political opponents and any person deemed "undesirable." In the camps, gas chambers were used for the genocide. There were mass shootings of Jews, and some were sent to gas chambers. In all, six million Jews were killed.

In all this persecution, anti-Semitism, discrimination, pogrom, and prejudice toward the Jews, they survived and built the state of Israel.

> For I know the plans I have for you says the Lord. "They are plans for good and not for disaster, to give you a future and a hope." (Jeremiah 29:11)

God has spoken, and nobody can change it. God says, "I know the plans I have for Israel, a plan of prosperity and a future, the Israelites hope for."

They were hoping for a homeland and a state of Israel. Building the state of Israel showed that the God of Abraham is still on His throne.

Theodor Herzl was the father of modern Zionism. He was born in May 2, 1860 in Pest, Hungary, in the Austrian Empire. He died on July 3, 1904, at the age of forty-four. He was buried in Vienna, Austria. In 1949, the Israelis requested his remains and gave him a resting place on top of Mount Herzl in Jerusalem. Theodor Herzl was a citizen of Austria-Hungry. He studied law at the University of Vienna and became a journalist, playwright, writer, and political activist. Herzl is mentioned in the Israeli Declaration of Independence and is considered the spiritual father of the Jewish state.

Other political activists were propagating Zionism and the state of Israel, but they were limited.

> Until Herzl came on the scene, Hovevei Zion could not attract mass support; it was just marking time. Herzl's sudden prominence, the preparation for the congress and the congress itself (reported by both Jewish and non-Jewish press), sparked the imagination of the Jewish masses and created for the first time a community of sympathizers for the Zionist idea.[7]

Among the pogrom, discrimination, and anti-Semitism of the Jews, the major problem for Herzl was the anti-Semitism, which Herzl tried to minimize. He fought very hard, but he did not live to see the achievement of his efforts. He died before the state of Israel was established.

Herzl used diplomacy to tackle his Zionist idea of a state of Israel. He negotiated with the Ottoman Empire,

---

[7] Anita Shapira, *Israel: A History*; Brandeis University Press, Waltham, Massachusetts, 21.

the German Kaiser, and the Russian minister of the interior, but none of his attempts were fruitful.

Ahad Ha'am, the leader of the Hovevei Zion movement, which was based in Odessa, criticized Herzl for using diplomacy. Ahad Ha'am thought the salvation of the Jews would come through the prophets and not diplomacy. Herzl met with the Russian interior minister, Vyacheslav von Plehve, but the meeting was unfruitful.

> The visit yielded nothing, but at the Vilna (Vilnius) train station Herzl met for the first time, crowds of Jews who had come to welcome him and demonstrate their sympathy with "the King of the Jews" and the idea of a Jewish state. Herzl was moved by the waves of love that flowed to him from the throng: this was a different Jewish experience, different from the restrain familiar to him in the Western Europe and from the angry reservations voiced by Ahad Ha'am and his followers. The violence displayed by the police who tried to disperse the crowds, and the people's bravery in the face of this brutality, perhaps made him feel committed to redeeming them, come what may.[8]

In *Der Judenstaat*, Herzl proposed Palestine and Argentina as places for a Jewish settlement, but he gave in to the proposal of British colonial secretary Joseph Chamberlain when he proposed part of East Africa, the area the

---

[8] Anita Shapira, *Israel: A History*; Brandeis University Press, Waltham, Massachusetts, 22.

Zionists called Uganda—present-day Kenya—for Jewish settlement. During the Sixth Zionist Congress, Herzl talked about the Uganda plan, but it was rejected by the Russian Zionist delegates. They considered it a betrayal of Zion and decided to split. They refused to rectify it. "Only when Herzl swore dramatically, 'If I forget thee, O Jerusalem, let my right hand forget its cunning,' did they agree to return to the congress hall."[9] In 1904, a year after the Uganda congress, Herzl passed away.

The Ottoman Empire had control over Palestine, and the British took control after it was crushed after World War I. In November 1917, the British government issued the Balfour Declaration, which announced plans to establish a home for the Jewish people in Palestine. On May 14, 1948, in Tel Aviv, David Ben-Gurion, the head of the Jewish Agency, proclaimed the state of Israel, establishing the first Jewish state in two thousand years. President Harry S. Truman recognized the new nation as a home for the Jewish people. In an afternoon ceremony at the Tel Aviv Art Museum, Ben-Gurion said, "We hereby proclaim the establishment of the Jewish state in Palestine, to be called Israel." Ben-Gurion became Israel's first prime minister.

The Arab countries came together to fight the newly formed state of Israel. Arab armies from Lebanon, Syria, Iraq, and Egypt launched an air strike on Tel Aviv, but the Israelites were able to resist the attack. Saudi Arabia sent an army under Egypt.

The Israelites had to fight a series of wars to keep the state of Israel, including the Six-Day War and the Yom Kippur War. The Israeli Defense Forces (IDF) holds a

---

[9] Anita Shapira, *Israel: A History*; Brandeis University Press, Waltham, Massachusetts, 23.

parade every Independence Day. This parade is held in a different city each year.

On May 15, 1967, Jerusalem hosted the parade. During the procession, a note was handed to the chief of staff, Yitzhak Rabin. After reading it, he passed it on to Prime Minister Levi Eshkol. Egyptian armored units had entered Sinai.

The Russians spread fake news that the Israelis were attacking Syria. Israel denied the news, and the American intelligence source also denied the news. It was not known why the USSR blew out such untrue and fake news. The Russians were only concerned about Syria, their loyal friend in the region. The Russians mobilized Egyptian aid to fight for Syria. Syria and Egypt had signed a mutual defense pact in 1996. The president of Egypt had to hold up his part of the bargain. Nasser was in a tight corner.

King Hussein of Jordan accused Nasser of hiding behind the UN peacekeeping forces at Sharm el-Sheikh and the Gaza Strip instead of assisting his Arab brothers. Nasser's top army officials thought they could defeat Israel and expel the UN Emergency Force (UNEF) in Sinai.

The UN secretary, U Thant, was asked to redraw the UNEF, and he agreed to the request. The Egyptian army was able to close the Straits of Tiran on May 23, 1967. Israel was trying to resolve this diplomatically, but their efforts were in vain. The Israelis were hoping the United States would come to their aid in case a war broke out, but President Lyndon B. Johnson had a lot on his hands. He was mired in the Vietnam War and was facing opposition at home.

On May 28, 1967, Eshkol's feeble speech caused the Israelis to demand a change of government. On June 1, 1967, a new government was formed. Menachem Begin was appointed minister without portfolio, and Moshe Dayan became minister of defense.

On June 2, 1967, the new Israeli government decided to go to war—after three weeks of waiting. On June 5, 1967, the IDF launched its offensive. The Egyptians were caught by surprise, and the entire Egyptian air force was destroyed. There were few Israeli losses, giving the Israelis air supremacy. They sent ground forces into the Gaza Strip and took over the Sinai Peninsula.

The Egyptian leader, Gama Abdel Nasser, told Syria and Jordan to join the fight.

Israeli counterattacks resulted in the seizure of East Jerusalem and the West Bank. They also took Golan Heights from the Syrians.

The battle ended on June 10, 1967, and the Israelis captured East Jerusalem, the West Bank, the Golan Heights, the Gaza Strip, and the Sinai Peninsula. It was a great achievement, and I believe the God of Abraham fought the battle for them. There was no way Israel could have won.

On June 11, 1967 a cease-fire was signed. The Arabs had lost more than twenty thousand forces, and Israel had lost less than one thousand. It was called the Six-Day war. Who really started the Six-Day War?

Although Israel fired the first shot against Egypt—although not against Jordan— the war was begun by Egypt's decision to close the Gulf of Aqaba to Israel shipping and to order the removal of U.N. troops from the Sinai. Although Israel fired the first shots, virtually everyone recognizes that Egypt, Syria, and Jordan started the war. The illegal Egyptian decision to close the Straits of Tiran by military force was recognized by the international community to be an act of war. As the Egyptian President Nasser himself boasted, "We knew the closing of the Gulf of Aqaba meant war with Israel ... the objective will be Israel destruction." The Egyptian commander of al-Shekh, the point of entry to the straits from which the Egyptians warned they would shoot at any Israeli ship that try to pass through on the way to and from Eilat, acknowledge that "the closing of the straits was a declaration of war." However, according to Nasser, the war was not to be over the Straits of Tiran but over Israel's existence. Nor was Israel's surrender contemplated. This, like the 1948 war, was planned to be a war of extermination.[10]

Yom Kippur is the most solemn religious fast of the Jewish year. The last ten days of penitence begin with Rosh Hashanah (the Jewish New Year). It is also known as the Day of Atonement, the holiest day in Judaism. Its central themes are atonement and repentance. During Yom Kippur, Jewish people spend the day in the synagogue, praying and fasting for forgiveness of sins and seeking God's face for the coming year.

The Arab coalition launched an attack on Israel during this day of fasting in 1973. The Yom Kippur War is also known as the October War or the 1973 Arab-Israeli War.

---

[10] Alan Dershowitz, *The Case for Israel*, John Wiley & Sons, Inc. Hoboken, New Jersey, 92.

The Arab States were led by Egypt and Syria. The war lasted from October 6, 1973, until October 26, 1973.

The fight mostly took place in the Golan Heights, and the Syrians were trying to take back the territory taken by Israel during the Six-Day War. The Israelis had to fight the Egyptian front from the Sinai Peninsula, along the Suez Canal.

Egyptian and Syrian forces crossed cease-fire lines and entered the Sinai Peninsula and the Golan Heights. Israel did not have a decisive win like the Six-Day War. The battle was a terrible one, and there were great losses on both sides. Although Israel was the winner, it came with a great loss of military personnel, manpower, and equipment.

On October 22, 1973, a United Nations-brokered cease-fire unraveled. Each side blamed the other for the breach. By October 24, 1973, the Israelis had nearly taken over Suez. This development brought tension between the United States and the Soviet Union, and a second cease-fire was imposed cooperatively on October 25, 1973, to end the war.

The war changed the face and policies of the Middle East. The Israelis were support by the United States, and the Arab Union was supported by the Soviet Union. The Arab Union—Egypt, Syria, Jordan, Iraq, Saudi Arabia, Libya, Tunisia, Algeria, Morocco, and Cuba—were supported by the Soviet Union, but the God of Israel did not allow the enemies to crush Israel. Israel had between 2,500 and 2,800 dead and 8,800 wounded. The total Arab coalition had between 8,000 and 18,500 dead and 18,000–35,000 wounded. The Israelites took the Arabs for granted, and the Arabs took them by surprise. Thanks be to the God of Abraham—for he did not allow the Arabs to crush Israel.

Has Israel denied the Palestinians statehood? Israel

has never done that, but the Palestinians have resorted to terrorism in the fight for statehood.

> The Palestinians never sought Statehood when they were occupied by Jordan and Egypt. Historically they wanted to be part of Syria. The claim of Palestinian to statehood began as a tactic to eliminate the Jewish state of Israel. Moreover, the Palestinian claim to statehood and Independence is no stronger, and in some cases far weaker, than the claims of the Tibetans, the Kurds, the Basque, the Chechens, the Turkish Armenians, and other stateless groups. Yet the Palestinian claim has been leapfrogged over other more compelling claims for one major reason: the Palestinians have attracted worldwide attention by murdering thousands of innocent people, whereas the Tibetans have never resorted to terrorism, and the other groups have employed only episodic local terrorism, which has not been rewarded by the international community in the way that Palestinian terrorism has been so richly rewarded. The Palestinian success in bringing their cause to the attention of the world has not, however, brought them a state, because neither Israel nor the United States has been willing to reward terrorism in the way the United Nations, the European Community, the Vatican, and others have.[11]

---

[11] Alan Dershowitz, *The Case for Israel*, John Willey & Sons, Inc. Hoboken, New Jersey, 164.

It is amazing to see two nations that were one-time enemies coming together to fight a common foe. According to thestar.com, in November 2017, the Egyptian affiliate of the Islamic State launched an attack, in which nearly forty gunmen stormed the al-Rawdah mosque in Egypt's sparsely populated Sinai region, killing more than three hundred worshippers. The terrorist group, which consists of more than one thousand members, first came to widespread public attention for its suspected role in the downing of a Russian airline in 2015, in which 224 people were killed. Egypt's military has struggled for years to destroy the group, which briefly seized control of the northern Sinai town of Sheikh Zuweid, and has launched dozens of attacks on soldiers, police, and Coptic Christian churches.

This group was operating between the border of Egypt and Israel. Israel could not tolerate the terrorist group on their doorstep and forged a secret partnership with Egypt to fight their common foe. According to nytimes.com, for more than two years, unmarked Israeli drones, helicopters, and jets have carried out a covert air campaign, conducting more than one hundred airstrikes inside Egypt—frequently more than once a week—with the approval of President Abdel Fattah el-Sisi.

The remarkable cooperation marks a new stage in the evolution of their relationship. Once enemies in three wars, then antagonists in an uneasy peace, Egypt and Israel are now secret allies in a covert war against a common foe. I hope this relationship will bring a lasting peace between Israel and Egypt.

According to BBC.com, on February 10, 2018, Israel inflicted damage on Syria's air defenses after one of its fighter jets was brought down during the raid over Syria. Iran is Israel's archenemy, and Iranian troops have been fighting rebel groups since 2011. Tehran has sent military advisers, volunteer militias, and—reportedly—hundreds of fighters from its Quds Force, the overseas arm of the Iranian Revolutionary Guards Corps (IRGC).

Iran is believed to have supplied thousands of tons of weaponry and munitions to help President Bashar al-Assad's forces and the pro-Iranian Hezbollah, which is fighting on Syria's side. Tehran has faced accusations that it is seeking to establish an arc of influence and a logistic land supply line from Iran through to Hezbollah in Lebanon.

Iran is trying to establish power and control in the Middle East, but Israel will not give in to any bully. When Iran sent a drone to Israel from Syria, the Israelis retaliated with an air strike in Syria. Following the air strike in Syria, Vladimir Putin urged the Israeli prime minister to avoid any action that could further escalate the confrontation. Benjamin Netanyahu said Israel had the right to defend its territory against any external aggression.

Is Israeli occupation the cause of all the problems? The Israelites are living in the place where their ancestors lived more than three thousand years ago. King David made Jerusalem the seat of its government in 1000 BC. To me, the Israelites are not occupying a territory. They are living in a place that belongs to them. I think the solution is a homeland for the Palestinians. If the Arab countries are real neighbors, then Jordan and Syria should be prepared to give a piece of their land to make a homeland for the Palestinians.

David Ben-Gurion was the first prime minister of Israel. David was a king of ancient Israel, when God selected Jerusalem to place His name and made Jerusalem the center of worship (spiritual and economic capital):

> But I have chosen Jerusalem that my name
> might be there; and have chosen David to
> be over my people Israel. (2 Chronicles 6:6)

David ruled over God's people in Israel more than two thousand years ago. I was not surprised that another David became the first Israeli prime minister. David Ben-Gurion was born on October 16, 1886, in Plonsk, Poland. He studied at the University of Warsaw, the largest university in Poland. Ben-Gurion also studied at Istanbul University in Turkey. Ben-Gurion was the founder of the state of Israel and the first prime minister of Israel.

Paula Munweis was born in Russia and raised in the United States. Ben-Gurion and Munweis met in New York and married in 1917. They were blessed with three children. Ben-Gurion's passion for Zionism propelled him to become the executive head of the World Zionist Organization in 1946. He was the head of the Jewish Agency from 1935 and later president of the Jewish Agency Executive. He was the de facto leader of the Jewish community in Palestine, and he led the struggle for an independent Jewish state in Mandatory Palestine.

On May 14, 1948, Ben-Gurion formally proclaimed the formation of the independent state of Israel and was the first to sign the Israeli Declaration of Independence. One of his major foreign policies was to improve Israel's relationship with Germany. He worked with Konrad Adenauer's government in Bonn, and West Germany provide large sums (in the Reparations Agreement between Israel and West Germany) in compensation for Nazi Germany's confiscation of Jewish property during the Holocaust. In 1954, he resigned as both prime minister and minister of defense, but he returned as a defense minister in 1955. In

1955, he became the prime minister again after elections. He stepped down from office in 1963 and retired from political life in 1970. He died on December 1, 1973, at Sheba Medical Center in Ramat Gan, Israel, and he was buried at Sde Boker, Israel.

The next prime minister is Golda Meir. She was a very important woman in Israel's history. The history of the establishment of the state of Israel would not be complete without Golda Meir. She was born on May 3, 1898, in Kiev, which is now Ukraine. Meir was a teacher, Kibbutznik, stateswoman, politician and the fourth prime minister of Israel. Moshe Mabovitch and Blume Neiditch were Meir's parents. Her father left Kiev in search of greener pastures in New York City in 1903. Her mother moved the family to Pinsk to stay with her mother.

Her father moved to Milwaukee, Wisconsin, and worked on the railroad. He was able to save enough money to bring his family to the United States. In Milwaukee, Golda Meir attended the Fourth Street Grade School, which is now Golda Meir School. After high school, her mother told her to marry, but she traveled to Denver to stay with her married sister, Sheyna. There, Meir was espoused to Zionism. She became a member of the Labor Zionist's youth movement. She spoke at public meetings and became a Socialist Zionist. She welcomed and hosted Jewish people from Palestine.

Meir married Morris Meyerson, and they left their lucrative jobs to join a kibbutz in Palestine. In her autobiography, *My Life*, Meir stated, "It is not only a matter, I believe, of the religious observance and practice. To me, being Jewish means and has always meant being proud to be part of a people that has maintained its distinct identity for more than 2,000 years, with all the pain and torment that has been inflicted upon it."

When Israel was established, the treasurer of the Jewish Agency was convinced that Israel would not be able to raise more than $8 million from American Jews, but Meir traveled to America and raised $50 million, which was used to purchase arms for the young country. Ben-Gurion wrote that Meir's role was as the "Jewish woman who got the money which made the state possible."

Meir was elected prime minister of Israel on March 17, 1969, after serving as minister of labor and foreign minister. To the world, she was the fourth Israeli prime minister, but to Israel, she was the first woman—and the only woman—to hold that post. She was described as the Iron Lady of Israel. Ben-Gurion used to call Meir "the best man in the government." She died on December 8, 1978, at the age of eighty.

Benjamin Netanyahu, the current prime minister, was born on October 21, 1949 in Tel Aviv. He was the first Israeli president to be born in Israel, to Israeli born mother, Tzila Segal, and a Warsaw-born father, Benzion Netanyahu. He was a second of three children. He is Israel's ninth prime minister and previously held the position between 1996 and 1999.

Netanyahu is a member of the Knesset and the chairman of the Likud Party. When Netanyahu was young, the family moved to the United States between 1956 and 1958 and again from 1963 until 1967. The family lived in Cheltenham Township, Pennsylvania, a suburb of Philadelphia. He attended and graduated from Cheltenham High School. After his high school graduation, Netanyahu returned to Israel to serve in the Israeli Defense Force. He served in the army for five years, and he was involved in several operations including Operation Inferno (1968),

Operation Gift (1968), Operation Isotope, and the rescue of the hijacked Sabena Flight 571 in May 1972 in which he was shot in the shoulder.

After serving the army for five years, Netanyahu returned to the United States to study at MIT). He majored in architecture. In October 1973, he returned to Israel to join the IDF in the Yom Kippur War. He returned to the United States to complete his SB degree in architecture in February 1975 and earned an SM degree from MIT's Sloan School of Management in June 1976. He worked as an economic consultant with a consulting group in Boston between 1976 and 1978. He met Mitt Romney at a consulting firm, and they became friends. He was studying toward his doctorate in political science at Harvard University, but he had to stop when his brother died in Operation Entebbe.

He lived in New York in the 1980s and met and became friends with Fred Trump, the father of Donald Trump. Netanyahu served as the Israeli ambassador to United Nations between 1982 and 1984. He served as deputy chief of missions at Israel's embassy in Washington from 1982 until 1984.

Benjamin Netanyahu has been married three times: Miriam Weizman (1972), Fleur Cates (1981), and Sarah Netanyahu (1991). In December 2006, Netanyahu became the official leader of the opposition in the Knesset and chairman of the Likud Party. In 2013, he became the second person to be elected to the position of prime minister for a third time, after Israel's founder David Ben-Gurion.

- 1996: minister of science and technology
- 1996: minister of housing and construction
- 2002–2003: minister of foreign affairs

- 2003–2005: minister of finance
- 2009–2013: minister of economic strategy
- 2009–2013: minister of pensioner affairs
- 2009–2013: minister of health
- 2012–2013: minister of foreign affairs
- 2013: minister of public diplomacy and Diaspora affairs
- 2013: minister of foreign affairs, minister of public diplomacy and Diaspora affairs
- 2015: minister of economy, minister of foreign affairs, minister of health, and minister of regional cooperation

> No weapon that is formed against thee shall prosper; and every tongue that shall rise against thee in judgment thou shalt condemn. This is the heritage of the servants of the Lord, and their righteousness is of me, saith the Lord. (Isaiah 54:17)

This is the assurance for the state of Israel since the God of Abraham will never leave the state of Israel alone. God will fight any battle or war for Israel. If all the Arab states come together with Russia supporting them, they cannot defeat Israel. God is fighting the war for Israel. Let the whole world form a coalition against Israel, and Israel will win the war because no one can fight with God and win. God the Almighty will be fighting for Israel. Any nation that goes against Israel will not prosper. It is better to be friends with Israel than to fight them.

Donald Trump, do not to be afraid to start building the American embassy in Jerusalem now. No weapon from any Republican, Democrat, or Independent against Donald

Trump shall prosper because God will fight his battle for him. At the end of this book, I will tell you, Mr. President, what you can do to win a second term. I know you will not like it, but I will be frank with you. Stop fighting your enemies. The battle is not yours. It is the Lord's. Do not fight Steve Bannon or anyone else who writes books about you. Leave it to God to fight for you. You need to change your attitude because you have a weird attitude. Learn how to speak diplomatically because you hold the highest post in the world. I will explain the difference between you and King Cyrus of Persia. He set the Israelis free from the Babylonian captivity and allowed them to build Jerusalem, the temple, and the walls of Jerusalem.

According to bbc.com, Israeli launched air strikes against Iranian targets in Syria after saying it had intercepted an Iranian drone crossing the Syria-Israel border. On February 10, 2018, Prime Minister Benjamin Netanyahu said his country would defend itself "against any attack" after carrying out what appeared to be its largest air strikes on sites in Syria.

Iran denies any allegations.

During the offensive, an Israeli F-16 fighter jet was shot down by the Syria air defense, crashing in Northern Israel. Its pilots ejected from the plane and were taken to the hospital. It is believed to be the first time Israel has lost a jet in combat since 2006. Mr. Netanyahu warned that Israel's policy to defend itself against "any attempt to harm our sovereignty" was "absolutely clear." "Iran brazenly violated Israel's sovereignty," he said: "They dispatched an Iranian drone from Syrian territory into Israel ... Israel holds Iran and its Syrian hosts responsible."

Mr. Netanyahu said Israel would oppose any attempts

by Iran to entrench itself military in Syria. During a meeting with military chiefs, he also said, "Israel seeks peace."

The US State Department said it supported Israel's right to defend itself, blaming Iran for the confrontation. In a phone call with Mr. Netanyahu, Russian President Vladimir Putin stressed the need to avoid a "dangerous escalation." He has been supporting President Assad's government in Syria's civil war. UN Secretary General Antonio Guterres has called for an immediate de-escalation in the actions that he said threaten a "dangerous spillover across Syria borders."

The confrontation between Israel and Iran could escalate if the United States and Russia do not come together and mediate between the two enemies. I believe no one can rouse the lion of the tribe of Judah without any consequences. I think it will be better for Iran to seek peace with Israel.

According to mobile.Reuters.com, Prime Minister Benjamin Netanyahu said on February 11, 2018, that Israel could act against Iran itself, not its allies in the Middle East, after the border incident in Syria brought the Middle East foes closer to direct confrontation. Iran mocked Netanyahu's tough words, saying Israel's reputation for "invisibility" had crumbled after one of its jets was shot down following a bombing run in Syria.

In his first address to the annual Munich Security Conference, which draws security and defense officials and diplomats from across Europe and the United States, Netanyahu held a piece of what he said was an Iranian drone that had flown into Israel airspace.

According to Fox News, a mysterious pool and fountain was discovered at an ancient Christian site in Israel. Archeologists in Israel announced the discovery of a large 1,500-year-old pool and elaborate fountain at the site of an ancient church near Jerusalem. The pool is a part of a system of pools unearthed at Ein Hanniya Park between 2012 and 2016. Built during the Byzantine era, the pools date back to between the fourth and sixth century BC.

Experts say that the capital is typical of royal structures found in the first temple period between 960 BC and 586 BC. The pool found in Ein Hanniya has been linked to the New Testament account of an Ethiopian eunuch's conversion to Christianity by Saint Philip the Evangelist. A Jerusalem District archeologist, Dr. Yuval Baruch, said, "We believe that some early Christian commentators identify Ein Hanniya as the site where the Ethiopian eunuch was baptized, as described in Acts 8:26–40." Israel is banking on tourism of Jerusalem and the surrounding environment.

> And the Angel of the Lord spake unto Philip, saying, Arise, and go toward the south unto the way that goeth down from Jerusalem unto Gaza, which is desert. And he arose and went: and, behold, a man of Ethiopia, eunuch of great authority under Candace queen of the Ethiopians, who had the charge of all her treasure, and had come to Jerusalem for to worship, Was returning, sitting in his chariot read Esaias the prophet. Then the Spirit said unto Philip, Go near, and join thyself to this chariot. And Philip ran thither to him, and heard him read the prophet Esaias, and said, Understand thou what thou readest? And he said, How can I, except some man should guide me? And he desire Philip that he would come up and sit

with him. The place of the scripture which he read was this, He was led as a sheep to the slaughter; and like a lamb dumb before his shearer, so opened he not his mouth: In his humiliation his judgment was taken away: and who shall declare his generation? For his life is taken from the earth. And the eunuch answered Philip and said, I pray thee, of whom speaketh the prophet this? Of himself, or of some other man? The Philip opened his mouth, and began at the same scripture, and preached unto him Jesus. And as they went on their way, they came unto a certain water: and the eunuch said, See here is water; what doth hinder me to be baptized? And Philip said if thou believest withal thine heart, thou mayest. And he answered and said, I believe that Jesus Christ is the Son of God. And he commanded the chariot to stand still: and they went down both into the water, both Philip and the eunuch; and he baptized him. And when they were come up out of the water, the Spirit of the Lord caught away Philip, that the eunuch saw him no more: and he went on his way rejoicing. (Acts 8:26–39)

One needs the Spirit of God to give a revelation to the Word of God. The eunuch was reading Isaiah 53:7–9, but the eunuch could not understand. If you seek God diligently, God will always provide a divine helper to assist you.

In the case of the Israelites in captivity in Babylon,

their divine helper was King Cyrus of Persia. For the eunuch of Acts 8: 26–40, his divine helper was Philip. Philip was able to explain to the eunuch that the prophet Isaiah was talking about Jesus Christ, the Son of God. He was led like a sheep to the slaughter and died for the sins of the whole world so that God could extend His election to the Gentiles. A person who believes that Jesus is the Son of God needs to be baptized, and that was why the eunuch was baptized.

A lot of sites in Jerusalem have significant importance to the Jewish and Christian faiths. The Jerusalem Wailing Wall is considered one of the holiest sites in the world. The Arabic word for the Wailing Wall is el-Mabka, which means "place of weeping." It has a significant place in Jewish history. At this location, the patriarch Abraham showed his devotion to God by his willingness to sacrifice his son Isaac. It is also believed that this was where Isaac went to pray before meeting Rebecca. At this same place, Jacob dreamed of a ladder reaching the heavens. It is believed that this was the very place where Solomon's temple or the Holy temple was built.

The temple was broken down when Nebuchadnezzar invaded Judah and burned Zedekiah's palace and the wall of Jerusalem. The temple was broken again during the Roman occupation of Judah. Christians believe the holy temple will be built there. The Temple Mount stands in the place where the holy temple for all nations will be built. God placed His name in Jerusalem during the reign of King David, and Jerusalem has played a pivotal role in Israeli and Jewish history ever since. Despite the destruction of the first and second temples, the presence of God has never left this place because God does not live in a building.

The Wailing Wall or Western Wall was built by King

Herod in 20 BC. Herod renovated many buildings and the temple to appease his subjects. People travel from all over the world to pray at the Wailing Wall. It is believed that every prayer done at the Wailing Wall is answered.

> And Solomon stood before the altar of the Lord in the presence of all the congregation of Israel, and spread forth his hands towards heaven: And he said, Lord God of Israel, there is no God like thee, in heaven above, or on earth beneath, who keepest covenant and mercy with thy servants that walk before thee with all their heart. Who hast kept with thy servant David my father that thou promisedst him: thou speaketh also with thy mouth, and hast fulfilled it with thine hand, as it is this day. Therefore now, Lord God of Israel, keep with thy servant David my father that thou promisedst him, saying, There shall not fail thee a man in my sight to sit on the throne of Israel: so that thy children take heed to their way, that they walk before me as thou hast walked before me. And now, O God of Israel, let thy word, I pray thee, be verified, which thou spakest unto thy servant David my father. But will God indeed dwell on the earth? Behold, the heaven and heaven of heavens cannot contain thee; how much less this house that I have builded? Yet have thou respect unto the prayer of thy servant, and to his supplication, O Lord my God, to hearken unto the cry and to the prayer,

which thy servant prayeth before thee today: That thy eyes may be open toward this house night and day, even toward the place of which thou hast said, My name shall be there that thou mayest hearken unto the prayer which thy servant shall make toward this place. And hearken thou to the supplication of thy servant, and thy people Israel, when they shall pray toward this place: and when thou hearest, forgive. (1 Kings 8:22–30)

This prayer continues to verse 61. In Chronicles, the Word of God declares that God answered Solomon's prayer with fire from heaven.

Now when Solomon had made an end of praying, the fire came down from heaven, and consumed the burnt offering and the sacrifices; and the glory of the Lord filled the house. (2 Chronicles 7:1)

That night, God also appeared to Solomon to confirm that Solomon's prayer had been answered.

And the Lord appeared to Solomon by night, and said unto him, I have heard thy prayer, and have chosen this place to myself for an house of sacrifice. If I shut the heaven that there be no rain, or if I command the locust to devour the land, or if I send pestilence among my people; If my people, which are called by my name, shall humble themselves, and pray, and seek my face, and turn from their wicked ways; then will I hear from heaven, and will forgive their sin, and will heal their land. Now my eyes shall be open, and mine ears attent unto the prayer that is made in this place. (2 (Chronicles 7:12–15)

God promised that He will answer any prayer that is made in this place from a clean and humble heart. Therefore, the wall that is left still carries the presence of God, so the prayer made at the Wailing Wall from a clean heart will be answered.

I hope to get the opportunity in the near future to go to Jerusalem and pray at the Wailing Wall.

3

MODERN-DAY
ISRAEL (PART B)

Israel is located between the southern shore of the Mediterranean Sea and the northern shore of the Red Sea. Israel is bordered by Lebanon in the north, Syria to the northeast, Jordan to the east, the Palestine territories of the West Bank, the Gaza Strip to the east and west, and Egypt to the southwest. There are two official languages in Israel: Hebrew and Arabic. Jerusalem is the capital and the largest city in Israel. Tel Aviv is Israel's economic and technology center.

The president of the United States recognizing Jerusalem as the capital is a great achievement for the Holy Land. In Israel, Jews form make up 78 percent, Arabs make up 21 percent, and others make up about 2 percent. The Holy Land is about 78 percent Jewish, 18 percent Muslim, 2 percent Christian, and 4 percent other.

Israel is a Democratic Unitary parliamentary republic. The 2008 listed a population of 7,412,200. In 2018, the census listed the population as 8,810,920, an increase of about 1.9 percent.

The total GDP for 2017 is $332.541 billion. For 2018, it is $361.609 billion ($40,762 per capita). There is an increase of the GDP within a year of 0.011 percent. The economy has been thriving. Hard work, intelligence, and trust in God of Abraham will see the nation through difficult times.

The change in Israel's economic character between the 1950s and 1990s can be summarized in the following facts; in the last decade of the twentieth century, only 2 percent of the working population was engaged in agriculture, and agricultural produce accounted for only 2 percent of the country exports. By the end of its first fifty years, Israel had been transformed a country whose symbol was the Jewish farmer plowing and sowing his field in accordance with the Zionist ideal into an industrialized country proud of its cutting-edge, high-tech industry. Despite limited water resources, optimal exploitation of those resources and the land enable Israel to provide food for its constantly growing population and even exports to Europe. But it is doubtful that the founding fathers of Zionism imagined that the return of the Jew to nature and physical labor would last no longer than two generations. In the 1990s Israel exports were based on industry and services, diamonds, tourism, and last on the list, agricultural produce. The economic revolution of the 1990s was marked by a shift from traditional industries such as textiles, machinery, construction, mining, and fertilizers to knowledge-intensive high-tech industries. The traditional industries were labor intensive, did not require a high level of specialization, and in most cases paid relatively low wages. The high-tech industries that flourished in the 1990s required higher education, a background in science or technology, and human capital. Their employees were individualistic, creative, and prepared to work hard for a relatively high salary. They made no long term commitment to the company, and the company made no commitment to its employees. The Israeli high-tech sector of the 1990s was in internet-related fields, life science start ups, and medical projects. Their success was the combined result of many years of investment in research and development, institutions of higher education that laid the scientific foundations for knowledge-intensive industries, and the influence of defense industries that invested in R&D projects in which a large number of first-generation high-tech entrepreneurs acquired their skills and ideas.[12]

Israel is widely known as the "start-up nation" and is recognized as a major player in the fields of innovation, R&D, and entrepreneurship. Like its American counterpart, Silicon Wadi is the area of high-tech concentration in Israel. *Wadi* is the Arabic word for valley. Silicon Wadi is the Silicon Valley of Israel, just like Silicon Valley in

---

[12] Anita Shapira, *Israel: A History*; Brandeis University Press, Waltham, Massachusetts, 449.

California. High-tech industries started in Israel in the 1960s. ECI Telecom started in 1961, and Tadrian and Elron Electronic Industries began in 1962. This company is regarded by many as the Fairchild of Israel.

Motorola, an American company, set up R&D in Israel in 1964. Motorola started developing wireless products, including remote irrigation systems and chips like the 68030.

The 1967 French arms embargo forced Israel to develop a domestic military industry, and military firms started to develop civilian applications for military technology. That brought in more innovation. Scitex Digital Printing Systems and Elscint developed innovative medical imaging and became leading forced in the market. At present, there are the Diamond Exchange District in Ramat, the Azorim High-Tech Park in Petah-Tikva, Yokneam's Startup Village High-Tech Park, Matam High-Tech Park in Haifa, Microsoft House in Herzliya, the Intel building in Petah Tikva, and the IBM building in Petah Tikva.

When the international computing industry shifted its emphasis from hardware to software products, Israel became one of the first nations to compete in the global software market. From 1984 through 1991, "pure" software exports increased from $5 million to $110 million. Many important ideas were developed by Mamram, Israel's computer corps, established by the IDF (Israel Defense Force). Israel has a leading edge in computer technology, which will boost the computer industry for years.

According to CNN.com, Germany has agreed to compensate Holocaust survivors from Algeria. This is good news. I really appreciate the German government for the Holocaust survivors. On February 5, 2018, Germany agreed to pay compensation to Jews who suffered persecution in Algeria during World War II. This is the first time that the Jews who lived in Algeria between July 1940 and November 1942 have been compensated by the German government for their suffering under the Nazi-collaborating French Vichy regime. Approximately twenty-five thousand people are eligible for a one-off payment of 2,556 pounds ($3,184).

The Conference on Jewish Material Claims against Germany negotiated with the German government on behalf of the Holocaust survivors. Germany's Ministry of Finance confirmed the agreement. The Claim Conference opened registration centers across France, where an estimated twenty thousand Algerian Jews reside, with the first payments expected to be made in July.

During World War II, northern France was directly occupied by Nazi Germany, and southern France was ruled by the Vichy regime. In Algeria, which was controlled by the Vichy government on behalf of the Nazis, Jews were stripped of their jobs in sectors such as education, media, and finance. They were prohibited from owning businesses, and their children were excluded from schools. Jews were banned from working for the government or military, and they were not allowed to work in businesses that had public contracts. Children were placed in segregated schools with Jewish teachers and older Jews. Jews were sent to labor camps to work on the Pan-Saharan railroad line. Camps were set up in Berrouaghia, Djelfa, and Bedeau.

It is amazing that the German government has acknowledged the suffering of the Holocaust survivors. Thank you, Angela Merkel, for the good work you are doing to console Holocaust survivors. I will be pleased if you follow President Donald Trump in declaring Jerusalem the capital of Israel and move the German embassy from Tel Aviv to Jerusalem.

4 DONALD TRUMP

According to CNN, President Donald Trump's approval rating hit 40 percent in a Quinnipiac poll on February 7, 2018, his best score in seven months. President Donald Trump has done well. The unemployment rate in July 2016 was 4.9, the unemployment rate in November 2017 was 4.1, and the unemployment rate in February 2018 was 4.1.

The economy is strong and steady. Healthy GDP data for the fourth quarter rounded off a strong year of growth in the economy. Household spending rose in the fourth quarter at a solid rate on continued job growth, increased wages, and high stock prices. Initial jobless claims continue to decline in 2018, and employment growth remained strong at the beginning of the year.

There was a brief federal government shutdown, but Congress struck a deal on January 22, 2018, to reopen the federal government through February 8, 2018. Congress failed to resolve the underlying issue that caused the shutdown, including an agreement on DACA.

President Donald Trump, please approve and sign the DACA deal without any strings attached to it. It will be a ticket for the next presidential election. America is full of immigrants from all over the world who are working hard to make America what it is now. The DACA kids are studying, and they are going to use their brain power to help make America great again. They will never forget that, during your time, they are approved and given a path to citizenship.

The unemployment rate is down by 0.8 since President Donald Trump took power. I believe it will go down more due to the strong economy. The strong economy is a feasible sign that President Donald Trump's government is building up the economy. It is believed that the economy will see a growth of 2.6 percent in 2018, and it is expected that it will be at 2.1 percent in 2019.

United States Economic Data

	2012	2013	2014	2015	2016	2017
Population (million)	314	317	319	321	323	
GDP per capita USD	51,386	52,705	54,502	56,175	57,436	
GDP (USD bn)	16,155	16,692	17393	18,037	18,569	
Economic growth (GDP annual variation percent)	2.2	1.7	2.4	2.6	1.6	
Domestic demand (annual variation in percent)	2.1	1.4	2.5	3.2	1.7	

Economic growth is expected to go up in 2018 due to the bold tax reform and other economic measures that have taken place. This can be checked at v.focus-economics.com. Tax reform is good, but corporations are going to benefit most. They will be able to create more jobs and bring down the unemployment rate. Dropping the corporate tax from 35 percent to 21 percent will put big money in corporations' pockets, but they will invest in the business and create more jobs to lower the unemployment rate. The low corporate tax will also attract foreign investors to the American economy. More jobs will be created, and the unemployment rate will be reduced.

The greatest thing that President Donald Trump has done is declare Jerusalem the capital of Israel.

> Pray for the peace of Jerusalem: they shall
> prosper that love thee. (Psalms 122:6)

President Donald Trump, you will see prosperity in your political career because of your love for Jerusalem and for declaring Jerusalem the capital of Israel.

President Donald Trump is the forty-fifth president of the United States of America. He has been in office since January 20, 2017. Trump was born in Jamaica Hospital in New York on June 14, 1946. His father was Frederick Christ Trump, and his mother was Mary Anne MacLeod Trump. His grandfather, Frederick, immigrated to New York City in 1885 from Kallstadt, Palatinate, which was part of the kingdom of Bavaria in the German Empire.

Frederick made a fortune in the Klondike Gold rush and returned to Germany to marry Elisabeth Christ, the daughter of a former neighbor. When Fred was born, the family moved to Woodhaven, Queens. Trump's grandfather died when Fred was twelve years old. At fifteen, Fred and Mary Anne began a career in home construction and sales.

The development company was incorporated as E. Trump and Son in 1927, and it build and managed single-family houses in Queens, barracks and garden apartments for navy personnel near major shipyards along the East Coast, and more than twenty-seven thousand apartments in New York. When Fred Trump died in June 1999, he was worth $250–300 million.

After graduating from New York Military Academy, Donald Trump went to Fordham University in New York between 1964 and 1966. He furthered his education at the Wharton School, which is the business school of the University of Pennsylvania, an Ivy League university located in Philadelphia.

President Donald Trump received five honorary degrees awards; the one from Robert Gordon University was revoked after Trump called for "a total complete shutdown of Muslims entering the United States" in December 2015.

- honorary doctor of laws from Lehigh University in Bethlehem, Pennsylvania (1988)
- honorary doctor of humane letters from Wagner College in Staten Island, New York (2004)
- honorary doctor of business administration from Robert Gordon University in Aberdeen, Scotland (2010) (revoked in 2015)
- honorary doctor of business administration from Liberty University in Lynchburg, Virginia (2012)
- honorary doctor of laws from Liberty University in Lynchburg, Virginia (2017)

President Donald Trump has also been recognized by many organizations. The following organizations have given recognition to President Donald Trump:

- Tree of life Award by the Jewish National Fund, for contributions to Israel-United States relations (1983)
- Ellis Island Medal of Honor in celebration of "patriotism, tolerance, brotherhood, and diversity" (1986)
- Golden Raspberry Award for Worst Supporting Actor, for portraying himself in *Ghost Can't Do It* (1991)
- Gaming Hall of Fame (1995)
- Star on the Hollywood Walk of Fame (2007)
- Muhammad Ali Entrepreneur Award (2007)
- WWE Hall of Fame (2013)
- The Algemeiner Liberty award for contributions to Israel-United States relations (2015)
- Marine Corps-Law Enforcement Foundation Commandant's Leadership Award (2015)
- *Sports Business Journal* most influential
- *Time* Person of the Year (2016)
- *Financial Times* Person of the Year (2016)
- Person in Sports Business (2017)

After graduating from Wharton, Trump started running the family's real estate business in 1971. Trump renamed the business the Trump Organization, which he expanded to involve constructing and renovating skyscrapers, hotels, casino, and golf courses. He managed his company until his inauguration as president of the United States of America on January 20, 2017.

Trump also gained prominence in the media and entertainment fields. He coauthored several books (most notably *The Art of the Deal*), and from 2003 to 2015, he was a producer and the host of *The Apprentice*, a reality television show. Trump owned the Miss Universe and Miss USA beauty pageants from 1996 until 2015. According to *Forbes*, he was the world's 544th richest person as of May 2017 with an estimated net worth of $3.5 billion.

> Surely the Lord God will do nothing, but he revealeth his secret unto his servants the prophets. (Amos 3:7)

Around 800 BC, God spoke through Isaiah to say that Cyrus—who was not yet born—would become king of Persia and deliver the Israelites from the Babylonian captivity. It happened as prophesied.

On Google, I found two prophecies about President Donald Trump. The first one was given by Kim Clement on April 4, 2007, in Redding, California.

> This that shall take place shall be the most unusual thing, a transfiguration, a going into the marketplace, if you wish into the news media. Where *Time* Magazine will have no choice but to say. *Newsweek* what I want to say. *The View*, what I want to say. Trump shall be come a trumpet, says the Lord. Trump shall become a trumpet. I will raise up the Trump to become a trumpet and Bill Gates to open up the gate of financial realm for the church, says the Lord. For God said, I will not forget 9/11. I will not forget what took place that day, and I will not forget the gatekeeper that watched over New York, who will once again stand and watch over this nation. Says the Spirit of God.

For I shall fill him with my Spirit when he goes into office and there will be a praying man in the highest seat in your land. There will be a praying President, not a religious one. For I will fool the people, says, the Lord. I will fool the people, yes, I will. God says, the one that is chosen shall go in and they shall say, "he has hot blood."

The Spirit of God says, yes, he may have hot blood, but he will bring the walls of protection on this country in a greater way and the economy of this country shall change rapidly, says the Lord of hosts.

Listen to the Word of the Lord. God says, I will put at the helm for two terms, but he will put at your helm for two terms, but he will not be praying President when he starts. I will put him in office and then I will baptize him with the Holy Spirit and my power. Says the Lord of hosts.

This powerful prophecy has come to pass. The prophecy showed that Trump would be elected president of the United States, and Donald Trump is now the president. The prophecy predicted that the economy would change rapidly, and the economy has done so. Donald Trump will bring a wall of protection on this country, and I believe America has seen peace. Donald will get his walls built on the Mexican border. The prophecy says Donald Trump will be put at the helm for two terms, which means Donald will win a second term and reign for eight years.

Another prophecy talked about the impeachment of Donald Trump, but the prophecy says nothing will come out of it. I think this is true since, so far, there is no evidence of collusion of Donald Trump's team with Russia.

How did this businessman turn into a politician? Before entering politics, Donald John Trump was a businessman and the host and producer of *The Apprentice*. Donald Trump was in the Reform Party from 1999 until 2001, was a Democrat from 2001 to 2009, and was an Independent from 2011 until 2012. He became a Republican in 2012 and used the Republican ticket to win the election in 2016.

When Trump entered the 2016 Republican primary, there were seventeen people. Trump had to defeat sixteen opponents to be the Republican nominee to meet the Democratic nominee, Hillary Clinton.

On June 16, 2015, Trump announced his intention to run for president at Trump Tower in Manhattan. In his speech, Trump drew attention to the most important issues—illegal immigration, offshoring of American jobs, the national debt, and Islamic terrorism—and made them his priorities during the campaign. He also revealed his campaign slogan: "Make America Great Again."

In the beginning, the race focused on Trump and Senator Ted Cruz. On Super Tuesday, Trump won the majority of votes and became the frontrunner for the rest of the primaries. After a landslide victory in Indiana on May 3, 2016, Ted Cruz and John Kasich suspended their campaigns.

The RNC chairman, Reince Priebus, declared Donald Trump the Republican nominee for the presidency. Trump won 14,015,993 votes to set a record for the most primary votes. The presidential race was between Hillary Clinton and Donald Trump.

Looking at the credentials of Hillary Clinton, there was no way Donald Trump, a businessman, could win.

Hillary Clinton had been the First Lady of the United States from 1993 to 2001. She was a senator for New York from 2001 to 2009. She was the sixty-seventh United States secretary of state from 2009 to 2013 and the Democratic Party's nominee for president in the 2016 election. With those credentials—and as the first female nominee—it seemed like it was going to be easy for her to win. I thought almost all the women and half of the men were going to vote for her. I did not know there was a prophecy that Donald Trump would win the election. That means God was fighting the battle for Donald Trump. I knew God was on Donald Trump's side as soon as he declared Jerusalem the capital of Israel. I knew that was why Trump won the election. Trump is the oldest and wealthiest person to be elected president of the United States of America. He is the first person without prior military or government service.

I believe Trump won the election because God wanted him to be president so that Trump would declare Jerusalem the capital of Israel and because Americans were tired of politicians who were in politics for their own interests and not those of the American people. Americans wanted a change.

Since Donald Trump became president, he has been able to take some bold decisions, which will be in the best interests of the American people in the long run. "Make America Great Again" is his yardstick for trying to do his best for Americans. In domestic issues, Trump got Gorsuch as the Supreme Court judge. Due to security concerns about ISIS and Al Qaeda, Trump did not want to take any chances with people from Muslim countries. He ordered a travel ban on citizens from several Muslim-majority countries. The first ban was rejected by the Supreme Court, but a revised version of the ban was implemented after a legal battle.

The tax reform bill was passed in December 2017, and it cut rates and eliminated the Obamacare insurance mandate. It is supposed to bring in more foreign investors since the corporate tax rate has been reduced from 35 percent to 21 percent. As more foreign investors come in, more jobs will be created, which may reduce the unemployment rate. The businesses that are here are going to get more money, which they will invest in businesses to create more jobs.

In foreign policy, Trump withdrew the United States from the Trans-Pacific Partnership trade pact and Paris Agreement on climate change, partially reversed the Cuban Thaw, pressured North Korea over the acceleration of their missile tests and nuclear weapons program, and recognized Jerusalem as the capital of Israel. Of all his foreign policy, the one that is amazing to me is declaring Jerusalem the capital of Israel.

Jerusalem has been a place of contention between the Palestinians and Israel. Even the European countries, the United Nations, and many other countries do not want to get involved in the tension over Jerusalem. I think Israel's claim to Jerusalem is more credible than that of any other country or state.

> But I have chosen Jerusalem that my name
> might be there; and have chosen David to
> be over my people Israel. (2 Chronicles 6:6)

Jerusalem became the spiritual capital and economic capital around 1000 BC. During the time of King David, God placed his name over Jerusalem. God said, "The place where I will place my name should be your spiritual/worship center and economic capital."

There is no country, people, or tribe on earth that can claim Jerusalem as their capital aside from the Jewish State or the state of Israel. I was so excited when President Donald Trump declared Jerusalem the capital of Israel. I am praying for the day that the world or the United Nations recognizes Jerusalem as the capital of Israel. Israel has the right to proclaim Jerusalem as its capital, and I am appealing to every country, nation, and state to recognize the right of Israel to select Jerusalem as its capital.

When Donald Trump became the president, I thought politics would be turned into business for Trump. He would know how to sell things that were made in the USA and the American brand. He has been able to do that before. Tax reform will bring in more investments. I know Trump to be a hard worker who knows what he wants. He loves talking about women on Howard Stern's radio shows, but he seems not to be a womanizer.

> For all of Trump's salacious chatter on the radio and carefully stage appearances with models and other beautiful women, those who spent lots of time with him through 1990s described not an overheated Casanova, but rather a workaholic and something of a homebody, a savvy business operator who was keenly aware of the value of being perceived as a player. Goldberg, the attorney who was often by Trump's side during those years, said many of his client's much-ballyhooed associations with famous women and top models were mere moments, staged for the cameras. "Give him a Hershey bar and let him watch television," Goldberg

> said. "I only remember him finishing the
> day [by] going home, not necessary with
> a woman but with a bag of candy. ... He
> planned his next project, read the blueprints
> met with the lawyers, never raising his voice,
> never showing off, never nasty to anybody
> in the office, a gentle man ... I never heard
> him speak romantically about a woman. I
> mean I heard him speak romantically about
> his work."[13]

Trump has also fought for religious freedom, which has
been under attack for so long. The evangelicals saw Trump
as a man of his word and voted massively for Trump.

> There were many who were surprised that
> Donald Trump enjoyed such overwhelming
> support from white evangelicals. After all,
> Trump isn't exactly the poster child for
> a devout Christian lifestyle. But I wasn't
> surprised. Trump pledged to protect
> religious freedom, which had been under
> unprecedented assault during the previous
> eight years. Evangelicals may not have
> believed Trump was a model Christian,
> but they believed he'd keep that promise.[14]

It is good to be a man of your word, and Trump is a man
of his word—and that helped to win the evangelical vote.

---

[13] Michael Kranish and Marc Fisher, *Trump Revealed*, Scribner, NY, 167.

[14] Michael Savage, *Trump's War*, Center Street, New York, NY, 215.

5 PRESIDENTIAL PROPHECY: DONALD TRUMP

Is President Donald Trump a born-again believer or a Christian? Is President Donald Trump baptized in the name of the Father, the Son, and the Holy Spirit?

At the end of Kim Clement's prophecy, he said, "Listen to the Word of the Lord. God says, I will put at your helm for two terms, but he will not be praying President when he starts. I will put him in office and then I will baptize him with the Holy Spirit and power. Says the Lord of Hosts."

Trump is going to be a praying President—but not right from beginning. When Trump ascended to the presidency, he was not a full-fledged Christian. As time goes by, he is going to see the need for prayers and turn out to be a strong, dedicated Christian who will be able to pray effectively.

His father's side was Lutheran, and his mother's side was Presbyterian. Trump's parents married in a Presbyterian church in Manhattan in 1936. When the family moved to Queens, they attended the First Presbyterian Church. Trump received his Confirmation there.

In 1970, Trump's family joined the Marble Collegiate Church (an affiliate of the Reformed Church in America) in Manhattan. The pastor, Norman Vincent Peale, author of *The Power of Positive Thinking* and *The Art of Living*, became the family pastor till his death in 1993. He was the mentor of Donald Trump. Trump is Presbyterian and has cited his mentor, Vincent Peale and his works during interviews when asked about the role of religion in his personal life.

If Trump backslid from his faith, there is a second chance for him to come back. I believe the love of money and his business life must have drawn him from his faith in Jesus Christ, but Jesus who is the Author and Finisher of our faith has given him a second chance to turn to him. Trump was treating woman as objects and not as human beings.

> For the love of money is the root of all evil: which while some coveted after, they have erred from the faith, and pierced themselves through with many sorrows. (1 Timothy 6:10)

Most of Trump's business deals might not be good if he could not show his taxes during the election, and the way he speaks and deals with people is unchristian.

> Who is a wise man and endued with knowledge among you? Let him shew out of a good conversation his works with meekness of wisdom. But if ye have bitter envying and strife in your hearts glory not, and lie not against the truth. This wisdom descendeth not from above, but it is earthly, sensual, devilish. For where envying and strife is, there is confusion and every evil work. But the wisdom that is from above is first pure, then peaceable,

gentle, and easy to be intreated, full of
mercy and good fruits, without partiality,
and without hypocrisy. And the fruit of
righteousness is sown in peace of them
that make peace. (James 3:13–18)

Trump has to deal with people with the wisdom that is
from above. It seems to me that he harbors bitterness and
strife within him, and it shows in the way he speaks and
deals with people.

I believe all of this can be changed. President Donald
Trump, before you do or say anything, think about if it
is going to bring peace. Will it bring peace—or are you
looking to satisfy your ego? It is not how powerful you; it
is knowing who you are in Christ. Your identity in Jesus
Christ is what every Christian should aspire to seek.
President Donald Trump, you should decrease and let
Jesus Christ increase in you.

The prophecy says you are going to be a praying
president—but not from the beginning of your office. To be
a praying president, you need to be a strong Christian who
is not moved by what you see or hear or the circumstances.
It is about your faith in Jesus Christ.

The challenges of being the president of the United
States of America will help you seek more of Jesus Christ
and let you be a praying president.

Kim Clement also talked about impeachment, but the
prophecy says it will not come true. President Donald
Trump, do not be afraid of what the enemy and his demonic
forces will do. Just pray and look unto Jesus, the Author
and Finisher of your faith.

You need to surround yourself with dedicated women
and men of God to pray with you. Prophetess Rosemond

Boateng of Harvest Fellowship International of Edison, New Jersey, is a woman of God. The words of this powerful woman never fall to the ground. I highly recommend this powerful woman of God to you. I also recommend my book *Effective Prayers* to teach you how to pray effectively and be a praying president.

Kim Clement's prophecy also talked about you coming in for a second term, and I believe it will come to pass. God has spoken, but the rest is on your shoulders. Do not make enemies for yourself—and be at peace with all men and women. Embrace people of color. You can be a father to all. Your actions speak louder than your words. Pray for your enemies and those who persecute you.

> Ye have heard it had been said, Thou shalt love thy neighbor, and hate thine enemy. But I say unto you, love your enemies, bless them that curse you, do good to them that hate you, and pray for them which despitefully use you, and persecute you; That ye may be the children of your Father which is in heaven: for he maketh his sun to rise on the evil and on the good, and sendeth rain on the just and the unjust. For if you love them which love thee what reward have ye? Do not even the publicans the same? And if ye salute your brethren only, what do ye more than others? Do not even the publicans so? Be ye therefore perfect, even as your Father which is in heaven is perfect. (Matthew 5:43–47)

President Donald Trump, Christians are to love our enemies. We do not fight them in public. We do not say nasty words that will create enemies for us. We do not fight our battles. We leave it for the Lord to fight the battles for us. All that we supposed to do is bring everything to the Lord in prayer.

Please learn to be a praying president instead of fighting unnecessary battles with words. I wish you would stop texting and battling with words. Be a praying president and fight everything in the spirit. It is spiritual warfare.

> For we wrestle not against flesh and blood, but against principalities, against powers, against the rulers of the darkness of this world, against spiritual wickedness in high places. Wherefore take unto you the whole armour of God; that ye may be able to withstand in the evil day, and having done all, to stand. Stand therefore, having your lions girt about with truth, and having on the breastplate of righteousness; And your feet shod with the preparation of the gospel of peace; Above all, taking the shield of faith, wherewith ye shall be able to quench all the fiery darts of the wicked. And take the helmet of Salvation, and the sword of the Spirit, which is the Word of God: Praying always with all prayers and supplication in the Spirit, and watching thereunto with all perseverance and supplication for all saints. (Ephesians 6:12–18)

According to these verses, there are two worlds. The spiritual world is controlled by God, and the evil side is controlled by Satan. The physical world is controlled by men and women (by the flesh). The physical world is controlled by the spiritual world.

God controls the spiritual and physical worlds, but God has given Satan and his forces permission to operate in this world till Judgment Day. Satan knows his time is limited, and he is doing everything possible to bring many people under his control and to their final doom.

The verses say we are not wrestling against flesh and blood, which means the fight is not against human beings. It is against principalities, which are the heads of the demonic forces that are assigned against heads of institutions, countries, states, and counties. They see to it that no good policies come out of any country or institution.

The next force Satan is using against us is power. Many people will be fighting to get power, and when they get it, the enemy will cause them to abuse the power. The next force is rulers of darkness, which includes wizards, witches, necromancers, psychics, and voodoo practitioners. Those forces rule the dark world.

The last force that the enemy is using to wage spiritual warfare against us is the wicked spirit in high places. These forces are very wicked. They have no sympathy, they are callous, and all they want to do is bring destruction to humankind. They are in high places. The only way we will be able to wage this spiritual battle is by putting on the whole armor of God.

The battle is not between us and any other human being. There is no need to fight back when people try to get you down. There is no need to text back if someone tries to assassinate your character. All we need to do to fight this battle is put on the armor of God and pray effectively. If you want to know how to pray effectively, you can read *Effective Prayers*.

What is the armor of God? The first armor is truth. We will do our best to be truthful in our dealings with others. The truth is like a belt on your pants, and if you do not put on your belt, your pants may come down, leaving you naked.

The next armor is the breastplate of righteousness. Righteousness is having the right standing with God. The blood of Jesus has given us the right standing with God. We need to keep this righteousness by living right with God. Read the Bible every day—and be prepared to abide or straighten your life with the Word.

The next armor is the gospel of peace. We have to read, live, and propagate the Word of God. When we live the gospel of peace, our lives and attitudes change to be like Christ. We need to talk about faith. We need to confess the Word of God every day in our lives and prayers. We need to confess the Word of God to the world so that those who do not know the Lord may come to know the Lord Jesus as Savior and Lord.

The next armor is the shield of faith, which the believer can use to protect himself or herself from the darts of the enemy. If you have been praying without seeing any results, the enemy will say, "Do you think God will answer your prayers?"

You will use your faith in the Word of God to say, "O thou that hearest prayer unto thee shall all fresh come" (Psalm 65:2).

You will say, "I know God answers prayers, and at the right time, he will answer me."

The next armor of God is the helmet of salvation.

Since the helmets are on our heads, we stand firm in our salvation so that the enemy may not get us.

> (For the weapons of our warfare are not carnal, but mighty through God to the pulling down of strong holds;) Casting down imaginations, and every high thing that exalteth itself against the knowledge of God, and bringing into captivity every thought to the obedience of Christ. (2 Corinthians 10:4–5)

This verse shows that this battle cannot be fought with our strength because our weapons are mighty and powerful through God and pull down every stronghold. God is fighting our battles. When God fights your battle, you never lose. You win all the time. You need to cast down everything that comes to mind that is not from God. That is why we need the helmet of salvation.

We need the sword of the Holy Spirit, which is the Word of God. We need the Word of God to guide us daily. We need to read the Word of God and abide by what we read. We need to put the Word into practice in our daily lives. We need to study the Word of God so that we can confess the Word of God when we are praying. It is easy to backslide if one is not well versed in the Word of God.

Why do we not fight the battle ourselves?

> Dearly beloved, avenge not yourselves, but rather give place unto wrath: for it is written, Vengeance is mine; I will repay, saith the Lord. (Romans 12:19)

There is no need to bother ourselves with what others are saying or doing to bring us down because the battle is not ours. If you get to know how to fight your battles, you will not need God to fight them for you.

If you are a believer, you do not fight your battles. If you pray, God will fight your battles for you. People may insult you, say nasty things about you, or accuse you of wrongdoing, but if you look unto the Lord, the Lord will fight your battle for you.

> To me belongeth vengeance, and recompense;
> their foot shall slide in due time; for the day
> of their calamity is at hand, and the things
> that shall come upon them make haste.
> (Deuteronomy 32:35)

Vengeance belongs to God. In due time, those who are fighting you will face the full wrath of God. It is not easy to let it go because your ego will prompt you to fight back when someone falsely attacks you. Just pray and leave everything in the hands of God. He will fight the battle for you.

6

THE PROS AND CONS OF KING CYRUS AND PRESIDENT TRUMP

There are some similarities in the lives of King Cyrus and President Trump.

- Isaiah prophesied about King Cyrus two hundred years before he was born. "That saith of Cyrus, He is my shepherd, and shall perform all my pleasure; even saying to Jerusalem, Thou shalt be built; and to the temple, Thy foundation shall be laid" (Isaiah 44:28). When Cyrus was born, the grandfather who was the king of the Medes wanted Cyrus to be killed because he had a dream where Cyrus had overthrown him.

- Kim Clement was a mighty man of God who prophesied about Donald Trump in 2007, almost nine years before Trump became president. On April 4, 2007, he said, "This that shall take place shall be the most unusual thing, a transfiguration, a going into the market place, if you wish into the news media. Where Time magazine will have no choice but to say. Newsweek what I want to say. The View, what I want to say.

Cyrus was given over to a shepherd who trained him for ten years. When he came back, the grandfather stopped chasing Cyrus. Cyrus grew up, overthrew the grandfather, and started building the Persian Empire. There was another prophecy on Cyrus. "Thus siath the Lord to his anointed, to Cyrus, whose right hand I have holden, to subdue nations before him; and I will loose the loins of kings, to open before him the two leaved gates; and the gates shall not be shut; I will go before thee, and make the crooked places straight: I will break in pieces the gate of brass, and cut in sunder the brass of iron: And I will give thee the treasures of darkness, and hidden riches of secret places, that thou mayest know that I,

Trump shall become a trumpet, says the Lord. Trump shall become a trumpet. I will rise up the Trump to become a trumpet and Bill Gates to open up the gate of financial realm for the church, says the Lord. For God said, I will not forget 9/11. I will not forget what took place that day, and I will not forget the gatekeeper that watched over New York, who will once again stand and watch over this nation. Says the Spirit of God.

- For I shall fill him with my Spirit when he goes into office, and there will be a praying man in the highest seat in your land. There will be a praying president, not a religious one. For I will fool the people, says, the Lord. I will fool the people, yes, I will.God says, the one that is chosen shall go in and they shall say, "he has hot blood."

the Lord, which call thee by name, am the God of Israel. For Jacob my servant's sake, and Israel my elect, I have called thee by thy name: I have surnamed thee, though thou hast not known me. I am the Lord, and there is none else, there is no God beside me: I girded thee, though thou hast not known me: That they may know from the rising of the sun, and from the west, that there is none beside me. I am the Lord, and there is none else" Isaiah 45:1–6. This prophecy was precise. The first prophecy gave the job description of what God wanted Cyrus to accomplish. Cyrus was to perform all the pleasure of the Lord. The Lord's pleasure was to free Israel from the Babylonian captivity. The assignment for Cyrus was to build Jerusalem.

The Spirit of God says, yes, he may have hot blood, but he will bring the walls of protection on this country in a greater way and the economy of this country shall change rapidly, says the Lord of hosts. Listen to the Word of the Lord. God says, I will put at the helm for two terms, but he will put at your helm for two terms, but he will not be praying President when he starts. I will put him in office and then I will baptize him with the Holy Spirit and my power. Says the Lord of hosts."

- God brought in Donald Trump because God wanted a good relationship between the United States and Israel.
- God wanted Donald Trump to declare Jerusalem the capital of Israel.

When Nebuchadnezzar captured Jerusalem, the whole city was burned down and needed to be built. When the foundation of the temple was laid by Zerubbabel, Cyrus died in a battle. Cyrus did not live to see the completion of the temple.

- God would cause kings to be afraid of Cyrus. God would loosen the loins of kings, which was the belt of the kings. The kings were going to be naked before Cyrus.

- God was going to open two gates. "God chose Cyrus, the king of Persia, to overwhelm kings, subdue nations and free Israel from their Babylonian oppressors. (On October 29, 539 BC, the priests of Madruk opened the gates of Babylon to the conqueror, and the city capitulated without raising a weapon).

- The American economy will be excellent and will rise up. The prophecy says the American economy shall change rapidly.

- Donald Trump will be in for the second term, and God will put Donald at the helm for two terms.

- Donald Trump will bring a wall of protection around this country. This should be a border wall between Mexico and the United States and getting assault rifles out of the market so that we will not witness Columbine, Sandy Hook, Parkland, or other mass shootings in our schools. I know you can do it President Trump. Please stop this carnage in the streets of America. There should be stricter gun laws that make it difficult for everyone, especially minors, to get guns.

- God said He would give Cyrus the treasures of the darkness and the hidden riches of secret places. This means God would provide wealth and riches for Cyrus to be able to build his empire, Jerusalem, and the temple.

- Cyrus was able to accomplish the task assigned to him. Cyrus conquered Babylon and set the Jewish people free from the Babylonian captivity. Cyrus allowed forty thousand Jews to leave Babylon and rebuild Jerusalem and the temple.

- Cyrus was a positive thinker and saw himself as a son of a great king.

- A charter portrayed what kind of person Cyrus was. A cylinder containing this charter was discovered in 1878 during an excavation of ancient Babylon.

- President Trump, we are looking at you to boost the American-Israeli relationship. Declaring Jerusalem the capital is a good start.

- Actions speak louder than words. I would like to see the character of Cyrus, which made him a father to all his subjects in his kingdom, being portrayed by

In this charter, Cyrus promised to treat all the inhabitants of Babylon and other kingdoms he conquered with respect. He swore that he would allow all inhabitants of his empire to practice their own religious and social customs without persecution. Cyrus also promised to punish anyone who acted cruelly to the religious and social minorities of his kingdom. Cyrus forbade the seizure of farmers' lands and properties and made slavery of any kind illegal. Cyrus's commitment to fair and equitable treatment of his people is exemplary by modern standards and was unique during his time period. Cyrus was called "the Father" because he was a father to all his people.

President Donald Trump. I want you to be called a father, just like Cyrus. You can do this when you build your relationship with African Americans, Hispanics, and Asians.

- Like Cyrus, please treat everyone with respect. Do not fight any group of people or text anything against any person or group.
- Cyrus allowed religious freedom and let minorities practice their social customs. I wish you would do so without any infringements of minorities in the United States.
- Please curb police brutality against minorities.
- Seek to be a praying president instead of a texting president.
- Please do not get angry over petty things because an angry person always makes the wrong decision.

7

A To-Do List for President Donald Trump

I would be very grateful if you could use all of your energy to get rid of guns from our country. Look at abccnews. go.com to see how assault rifles have played a prominent role in American mass shootings.

> Americans are grappling with yet another massacre after a Texas church's Sunday morning services were interrupted by a gunman who sprayed parishioners with bullets from an AR-15 platform rifle. Air Force veteran Devin Kelly killed 26 people—many of them children—and left 20 other people injured, in what authorities have called a domestic situation.

Let us look at school shootings and the number of people being killed. Young, vibrant students are being killed at the primes of their lives because Congress and executives are afraid of the National Rifle Association. They refuse to take assault rifles off the market. Many members of Congress support the NRA.

Even someone who is mentally ill is able to get a gun

without any scrutiny. Many people only think about themselves and the money they are making from the sales of assault rifles. They do not care if our children are being killed so they can make money. There have been so many school shootings since 1960:

- The University of Texas : On August 1, 1966, Charles Whitman, a former marine sharpshooter, opened fire from the observation deck on a tower of the University of Texas at Austin. He killed thirteen people, including one unborn child, and thirteen people were injured.

- Columbine High School. On April 20, 1999, at Columbine High School in Colorado, Eric Harris and Dylan Klebold shot and killed twelve students and one teacher. Twenty-one people were injured, and three people were injured while trying to escape.

- Virginia Tech. On April 16, 2007, Seung-Hui Cho, a senior at Virginia Tech, shot and killed thirty-two people and wounded seventeen people.

- Sandy Hook Elementary School. On December 14, 2012, in Newtown Connecticut, twenty-year-old Adam Lanza fatally shot and killed twenty children and six adult staff members. He killed his mother before setting off to the elementary school. He committed suicide as the first responders arrived on the scene.

- Marjory Stoneman Douglas High School. Parkland, Florida, witnessed the deadliest school shootings in American history on February 14, 2018. Nikolas Cruz shot and killed seventeen people, including students and staff members. Another fourteen students were hurt. He was able to get away by blending in with fleeing students, but authorities were able to arrest him as he was walking down a residential street.

President Donald Trump, you are the hope of all Americans. If you are bold enough to declare Jerusalem the capital of Israel, then be bold enough to enforce tougher gun laws. Please enact a law that will make it difficult for assault rifles to be on the market. Israel has good policies on guns and tougher gun laws—why not learn from Israel? Tough laws will not allow mentally ill people to get guns. If a mentally ill person lives in a residence, that residence should get rid of all its guns. Every school should have metal detectors and search student bags. Please do something to stop the killing of innocent children. There should be gun control, and AR-15s and other assault rifles should not be on the market. Gun control will be welcome.

Please, President Donald Trump, your name will go into the history books as the best president ever if you are able to enforce tougher gun laws. You will be able to protect a lot of Americans—even unborn Americans. Do not relax and allow the gun lobby to dissuade you. If you want to make America great again, then enforce tougher gun laws. Tougher gun laws will be your ticket for the second term.

We need a common-sense gun laws to make America great again. On the news in Philadelphia, I heard about a principal who told his kids that if there were no fights or other violence for the entire school year, each kid would receive one hundred dollars. It worked like magic. Everyone wanted to get the money, and the violence and school fighting ceased. Please do what it takes to make our schools safer.

Make America great again by enforcing tougher gun laws. Those who have taken millions of dollars from the NRA will say tougher gun laws will not work, but that is a lie. They are protecting their own interests. Do not listen to them.

CNN said there have been twenty-one mass murders in the twenty years since the Columbine High School massacre. That is unacceptable, and something needs to be done. I believe you have the boldness and courage to sanction tougher gun laws. Please look unto Jesus Christ, the Author and Finisher of our faith, and not at what the NRA is saying. We need tougher gun laws. The *New York Post* writes, "Mr. President, it's time to do something about guns. President Trump plainly feels the nation's grief and anger over young Nikolas Cruz's shooting rampage at Marjory Stoneman Douglas High School. The question is: Will he seize the chance to do something about mass shootings?"

Tuition at higher institutions is skyrocketing. If the administrators are not prepared to do something about the cost of education, then I think you can. President Donald Trump, you can create a ceiling that no school can pass for tuition. The federal government can also provide more grants and scholarships for deserving students to make education possible for more Americans. The percentage on student loans could be as low as 2 percent to attract more people to school. The best percentage on student loans are between 3.25 percent and 3.46 percent. This high rate favors the loan companies, and they are making more money. I believe the federal government needs to do something about tuition. President Trump, the kids need to go to school and graduate to make America great again. Education is the yardstick that makes America great again.

The health system is the next on the agenda. This is

not about Obamacare. It is about creating a competitive health insurance policy so that more Americans will be able to afford health insurance. I do not know how, but if you bring together the good minds from the Democrats and Republicans, it will get us good health care. Healthy Americans will be able to work hard to make America great again. We need to take good care of the young, the disabled, and the elderly with good insurance. The veterans also need good medical care. A nation that is able to cater to the old, the young, the disabled, and the veterans will surely be great.

The DACA and immigration laws are the next on the list. I know the Senate rejected three proposals from President Donald Trump that could have made the Dreamers get protected legal status on February 15, 2018. Please, Mr. President, do your best to bring both parties together to draft a better proposal that will appeal to both parties and resolve the DACA situation once and for all.

You need to protect America from terrorists and make this country great again. You will need tougher immigration laws, but do not forget those who are already in the system. The FBI, ICE, and police forces know which immigrants are here to work and which are bad apples. Let the good, hardworking immigrants get their papers and continue to work hard to make America great. You can flush the bad ones out of the system. I do not believe in rewarding people for bad work, but a reward is good for good work.

Mr. President, it is my prayer that the Holy Spirit will guide you and give you wisdom in making wise decisions to make America great again. I know many people will be mad about what I want you to implement in the elementary and high schools all over America.

> The wicked shall be turned into hell, and all
> the nations that forget God. (Psalms 9:17)

Please do not get me wrong. I do not want the United States to forget God. Morning prayers and worship were part of elementary and high schools in the United States. On June 25, 1962, the United States Supreme Court decided in *Engel v. Vitale* that prayer approved by the New York Board of Regents for use in schools violated the First Amendment because it represented the establishment of religion. According to cnsnews.com, in 1963, in *Abington School District v. Schempp*, the court decided against Bible reading in public schools along the same lines.

Since 1963, Jeynes said there have been five negative developments in the nation's public schools:

- academic achievement has plummeted, including SAT scores
- increase in rate of out-of-wedlock births
- increase in illegal drug use
- increase in juvenile crime
- deterioration of school behavior
- increase in rate of school shootings

According to the *Washington Times*,

> The White House was able to bring Israelis and the Arab States diplomats for the first time to a table talk conference on Tuesday March 13, 2018, in discussing the humanitarian crisis in Gaza.
>
> The six-hour meeting in the White House was hosted by senior presidential

advisor Jared Kushner and Jason Greenblatt, the president's special representative for the Middle East talks. A total of twenty countries attended including Israel, Saudi Arabia, Jordan, United Arab Emirates, Qatar, France, the United Kingdom, Germany, as well as representatives from the United Nations and Europe Union.

"The situation in the Gaza must be solved for humanitarian reasons and ensuring the security of Egypt and Israel," the White House said in a statement Wednesday. "It is also necessary step towards reaching a comprehensive peace agreement between the Israelis and the Palestinians, including the Palestinians in both Gaza and the West Bank.

This is remarkable achievement for President Donald Trump. He has proven himself to be a modern-day Cyrus.
According to the BBC,

President Donald Trump has warned Syria's government the US is "locked and loaded" to strike again if it carries out chemical attacks.

The warning came after the US, UK and France struck three Syrian sites in response to a suspected deadly chemical attack in the town of Duma a week ago. Syria denies any chemicals used and says that the attack was fabricated by rebels

> A UN Security Council resolution
> voted brought by Syria's ally, Russia, to
> condemn the US-led strikes was rejected.

What leader in this modern world in his or her right frame of mind would support President Bashir Assad's government for slaughtering more than half a million Syrians through conventional and chemical weapons? Bashir Assad has proven himself to be a modern-day Hitler. The UK prime minister, Theresa Mary May, and the president of France, Emmanuel Macron made a wise decision in supporting Donald Trump to accomplish the mission. Syria is an enemy.

President Donald Trump, I believe God has a purpose for making you the president of the United States of America.

> And he changeth the times and the
> seasons: he removeth kings, and setteth
> up kings: he giveth wisdom unto the
> wise, and knowledge to them that know
> understanding. (Daniel 2:21)

God sets up presidents and removes presidents. I want you to know that God brought you to this seat for a purpose. One of the purposes is for you to restore Bible teachings, readings, and prayers in elementary and high schools.

> Train up a child in the way he should go:
> and when he is old, he will not depart from
> it. (Proverbs 22:6)

If you do not train your child, the child will pick a disastrous way and may shoot his or her classmates. Prayers and Bible studies in schools will improve the moral standards of the kids, and they will grow up to be responsible human beings who will make America great again.

God brought you to this seat to bring stricter gun regulations and stop the mass killings in this country. I thank you for proclaiming Jerusalem as the capital of Israel, and I think this is the main reason why God brought you to power.

> This that shall take place shall be the most unusual thing, a transfiguration, a going into the market place, if you wish into the news media. Where *Time* magazine will have no choice but to say. *Newsweek* what I want to say. *The View*, what I want to say. Trump shall become a Trumpet, says the Lord. Trump shall become a trumpet. I will rise up the Trump to become a trumpet and Bill Gates to open up the gate of financial realm for the church, says the Lord. For God, said I will not forget 9/11. I will not forget what took place that day, and I will not forget the gatekeeper that watched over New York, who will once again stand and watch over this nation. Says the Spirit of God. For I shall fill him with my Spirit when he goes into office and there will be a praying man in the highest seat in your land. There will be a praying President, not a religious one. For I will fool the people, says, the Lord. I will fool the people, yes, I will. God says, the one that is chosen shall go in and they shall say, "he has hot blood." The Spirit of

> God says, yes, he may have hot blood, but he will bring the walls of protection on this country in a greater way and the economy of this country shall change rapidly, says the Lord of hosts.
>
> Listen to the Word of the Lord. God says, I will put at the helm for two terms, but he will put at your helm for two terms, but he will not be praying President when he starts. I will put him in office and then I will baptize him with the Holy Spirit and my power. Says the Lord of hosts.

This amazing prophecy mentions how media like *Time* magazine says what God wants them to say about Trump. *Time* named President Donald Trump its Person of the Year in 2016. *Sports Journal* also saw President Trump as the most influential person of 2016. President Trump was also named the *Financial Times* Person of the Year in 2016. The prophecy was on point.

The prophecy said that God will raise a gatekeeper who will watch over New York. I believe God has done that since New York has seen peace since 9/11. God has said the gatekeeper will continue to watch over New York. The prophecy declared that Trump would bring a wall of protection around this country—a wall between Mexico and the United States.

I think Trump will be a praying president. President Trump, if you have not started praying, this is the time to start. Please do a Bible study each morning and pray before your morning duties. You are going to see the difference. Stop texting and fighting your own battles. Leave everything in the hands of God.

The prophecy said that God would baptize you with the Holy Spirit, which means you are going to be a Pentecostal Christian who will speak in tongues. Isaiah prophesied the outpouring of the Spirit: "Until the spirit be pour upon us from on high, and the wilderness be a fruitful field, and fruitful field be counted for a forest" (Isaiah 32:15).

A person who does not know Jesus as a Savior and Lord is in the wilderness. There is nothing good in the wilderness. When that person accepts Jesus as Savior and Lord, the Spirit of God is poured from on high and takes residence in the person. The person becomes a fruitful field. When the person gets to know more of God and desires to decrease for Christ to increase, the person will be baptized in the Holy Spirit, will start speaking in tongues, and will be counted as a forest.

> And, behold, I send the promised of my Father upon you: but tarry ye in the city of Jerusalem, until ye be endue with power from on high. (Luke 24:49)

Jesus was talking about the disciples being imbued with power from on high. It was being baptized with the Holy Spirit.

> But ye shall receive power, after that the Holy Spirit is come upon you: and ye shall be witnesses unto me both in Jerusalem, and in all Judea and in Samaria, and unto the uttermost part of the earth. (Acts 1:8)

On the day of Pentecost, the disciples were baptized with the Holy Spirit and spoke in tongues. The disciples were commissioned to evangelize unto the uttermost part of the earth, which is throughout the world. The election of God was open to the Gentiles. God had a plan when Satan took over the Garden of Eden. God called Abraham and blessed him. The election of God started with Abraham and his descendants, the Jews, and the seed of Abraham. Jesus Christ came so that God's election would be open to the world.

To make America great again, President Donald Trump needs to do certain things.

- I think you should know Jesus—then it is time for you to be a praying President.
- Do not forget to build a good relationship with Israel and build the US embassy in Jerusalem in time to back your words with action.
- Please restore prayers and Bible reading in the schools.
- There should be stricter regulations on guns.
- Do your best to build a good relationship with minorities.
- Stop texting and leave the Lord to fight your battles.
- Let the women see their wealth in society and treat them with respect.

I am sure the Lord Jesus will give you the strength and power to be strong enough to make America great again.

BIBLIOGRAPHY

Lamb, Harold, *Cyrus the Great*, Doubleday & Company, Inc., Garden City, NY.

Walton, John H., *Ancient Near Eastern Thought and the Old Testament*, Baker Academic, Grand Rapids, Michigan.

Wiesehofer, Josef, *Ancient Persia*, I. B. Tauris Publishers New York.

Shapira, Anita, *Israel: A History*, Brandeis University Press, Waltham, Massachusetts.

Dershowitz, Alan, *The Case for Israel*, John Wiley & Sons, Hoboken, New Jersey.

Kranish, Michael and Marc Fisher, *Trump Revealed*, Scribner, New York.

Savage, Michael, *Trump's War*, Center Street, New York.

Paul, Shalom M., *Eerdmans Critical Commentary*; Wm. B. Eerdmans Publishing Co. Grand Rapids, Michigan.

Britannica.com

Wikipedia

Study.com

Politico.eu

thestar.com

nytimes.com

bbc.com

abccnews.go.com

New York Times

cnsnews.com

Fox News

cnn.com
mobile.Reuters.com
v.focus_economics.com
Jerusalem Post